SOUTHEND

A POCKET ALBUM

Adapted from an original book by
FRANCES CLAMP

First published in the United Kingdom in 2004 by
Frith Book Company Ltd

ISBN 1-85937-822-6

Text and Design copyright © Frith Book Company Ltd
Photographs copyright © The Francis Frith Collection

The Frith photographs and the Frith logo are reproduced under licence from Heritage
Photographic Resources Ltd, the owners of the Frith archive and trademarks

British Library Cataloguing in Publication Data

Southend - A Pocket Album
Adapted from an original book by Frances Clamp

Frith Book Company Ltd
Frith's Barn, Teffont,
Salisbury, Wiltshire SP3 5QP
Tel: +44 (0) 1722 716 376
Email: info@francisfrith.co.uk
www.francisfrith.co.uk

Printed and bound in Great Britain by MPG, Bodmin

Front Cover: **CANVEY ISLAND,** A Beach Scene c1955 / C237065

Frontispiece: **SOUTHEND,** The Boating Lake c1950 / S155020

The colour-tinting is for illustrative purposes only, and is not intended to be historically accurate.

AS WITH ANY HISTORICAL DATABASE THE FRITH ARCHIVE IS CONSTANTLY
BEING CORRECTED AND IMPROVED AND THE PUBLISHERS WOULD
WELCOME INFORMATION ON OMISSIONS OR INACCURACIES

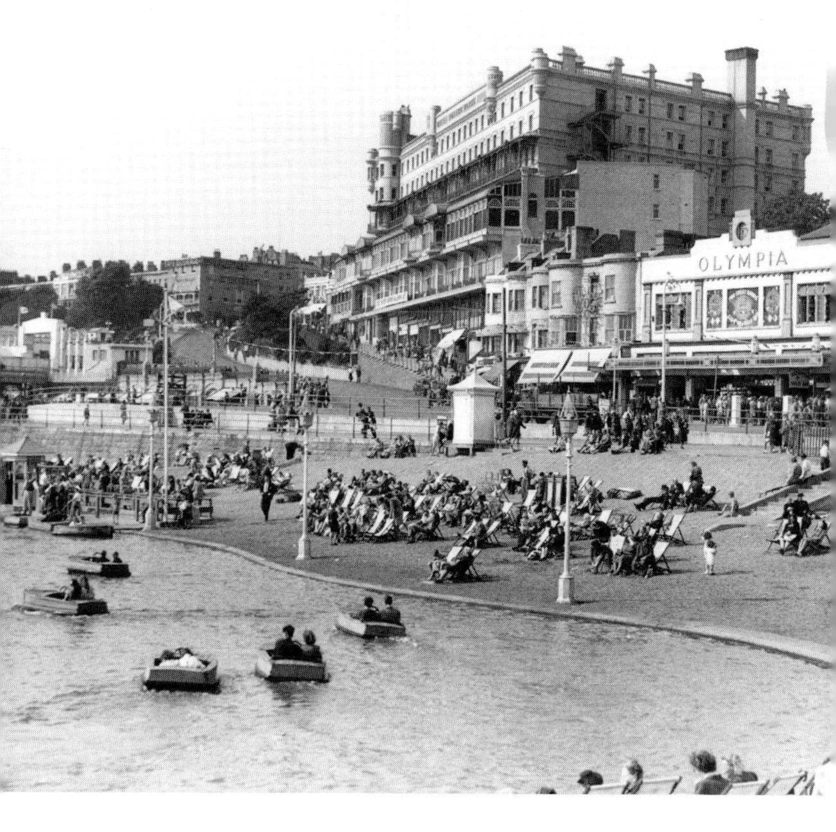

FRANCIS FRITH'S *pocket* ALBUM

Keep this pocket-sized Frith book with you when you are visiting Southend, or if you are on holiday in the locality.

Whether you are in your car or on foot, you will enjoy an evocative journey back in time. Compare the Southend of old with what you can see today— see how the streets of the town and its parks and open spaces have changed; experience the Great British Holiday as it once was—the fun and frivolity of the seafront, with its beach and famous pier; examine the hotels, shops and buildings in and around the town and notice how they have been altered or replaced; and see the many alterations to Southend and its surrounding villages that have taken place unnoticed during our lives, some of which we may have taken for granted.

At the turn of a page you will gain fascinating insights into Southend's unique history.

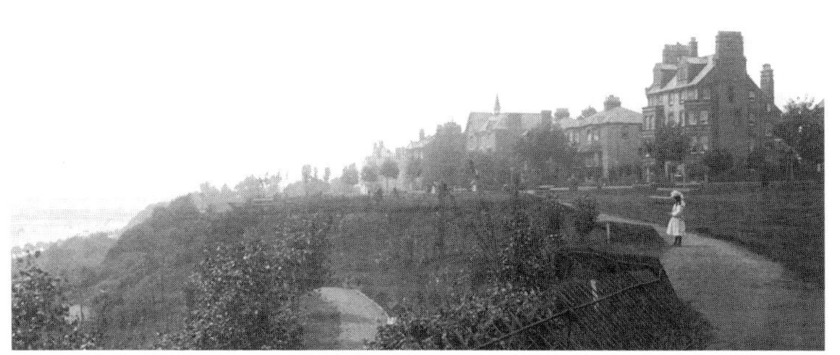

CONTENTS

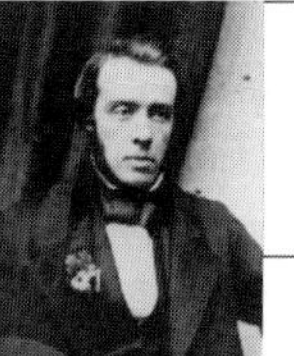

FRANCIS FRITH
VICTORIAN PIONEER

Francis Frith, founder of the world-famous photographic archive, was a complex and multi-talented man. A devout Quaker and a highly successful Victorian businessman, he was philosophical by nature and pioneering in outlook. By 1855 he had already established a wholesale grocery business in Liverpool, and sold it for the astonishing sum of £200,000, which is the equivalent today of over £15,000,000. Now in his thirties, and captivated by the new science of photography, Frith set out on a series of pioneering journeys up the Nile and to the Near East.

INTRIGUE AND EXPLORATION

He was the first photographer to venture beyond the sixth cataract of the Nile. Africa was still the mysterious 'Dark Continent', and Stanley and Livingstone's historic meeting was a decade into the future. The conditions for picture taking confound belief. He laboured for hours in his wicker dark-room in the sweltering heat of the desert, while the volatile chemicals fizzed dangerously in their trays. Back in London he exhibited his photographs and was 'rapturously cheered' by members of the Royal Society. His reputation as a photographer was made overnight.

VENTURE OF A LIFE-TIME

By the 1870s the railways had threaded their way across the country, and Bank Holidays and half-day Saturdays had been made obligatory by Act of Parliament. All of a sudden the working man and his family were able to enjoy days out, take holidays, and see a little more of the world.

With typical business acumen, Francis Frith foresaw that these new tourists would enjoy having souvenirs to commemorate their days out. For the next thirty years he travelled the country by train and by pony and trap, producing fine photographs of seaside resorts and beauty spots that were keenly bought by millions of Victorians. These prints were painstakingly pasted into family albums and pored over during the dark nights of winter, rekindling precious memories of summer excursions. Frith's studio was soon supplying retail shops all over the country, and by 1890 F Frith & Co had become the greatest specialist photographic publishing company in the world, with over 2,000 sales outlets, and pioneered the picture postcard.

FRANCIS FRITH'S LEGACY

Francis Frith had died in 1898 at his villa in Cannes, his great project still growing. The archive he created continued in business for another seventy years. By 1970 it contained over a third of a million pictures showing 7,000 British towns and villages.

Frith's legacy to us today is of immense significance and value, for the magnificent archive of evocative photographs he created provides a unique record of change in the cities, towns and villages throughout Britain over a century and more. Frith and his fellow studio photographers revisited locations many times down the years to update their views, compiling for us an enthralling and colourful pageant of British life and character.

We are fortunate that Frith was dedicated to recording the minutiae of everyday life. For it is this sheer wealth of visual data, the painstaking chronicle of changes in dress, transport, street layouts, buildings, housing, engineering and landscape that captivates us so much today, offering us a powerful link with the past and with the lives of our ancestors.

Computers have now made it possible for Frith's many thousands of images to be accessed almost instantly. The archive offers every one of us an opportunity to examine the places where we and our families have lived and worked down the years. Its images, depicting our shared past, are now bringing pleasure and enlightenment to millions around the world a century and more after his death.

SOUTHEND
AN INTRODUCTION

The smell of fish and chips, candy floss and seaweed; the sound of slot machines, motorbikes, bingo callers and fairground rides; the sight of the longest pleasure pier in the world; jostling crowds and children playing on the beach - this is the usual image of Southend-on-Sea. Yet there is more - so much more - to this popular seaside town.

The Coat of Arms tells something of the history of the town. The motto, Per Mare per Ecclesiam (By the Sea and by the Church) relates the two great influences that have affected the whole of the Southend area. As well as a monk and a medieval fisherman, there are also symbols of the four ancient parishes of Prittlewell, Leigh, Eastwood and Southchurch, each with its own fascinating history and all later incorporated into the borough.

In the Middle Ages a priory, parish church and village flourished close to the Prittle Brook. At the south end of this community, near to the sea, stood a few fishermen's huts. This was further to the east than the present centre of the town and the pier, but was the beginning of the town later to be known as Southend-on-Sea.

It was during the reign of Henry I that a Cluniac priory was first established at Prittlewell, although there had been settlement in the area long before that, as was proved when a Saxon cemetery was discovered close by in 1923. Spears, swords and jewellery were found. It is thought that St Cedd may have built a church at Prittlewell, after re-establishing Christianity in the region in AD653. Artefacts from the area can be seen in the Southend-on-Sea Central Museum.

Leigh was a thriving medieval port. Many of the weatherboard cottages of Old Leigh still remain, having fortunately escaped the road development planned in the late 1940s. A fire at The Peter Boat Inn in 1892 revealed an interesting aspect of the town's past. A secret chamber was discovered, a smugglers' store from bygone days. The distinctive smell from the cockle sheds has assailed the noses of generations of visitors to the town.

Eastwood was mentioned in the Domesday Book. The entry is recorded on the wall in the parish church of St Lawrence.

Holy Trinity is the Parish Church of Southchurch. Although parts of the building are Norman, it is known that an earlier church existed here in the 9th century. Southchurch was also mentioned in the Domesday Book, with both fishing and agriculture being important at that time. The original parish boundaries included the whole of Thorpe Bay.

Stratsende or Strateshend is first recorded early in the 14th century. Meaning 'the end of the street' this is possibly the first mention of Southend. This 'street' probably ran between Prittlewell and Milton, a hamlet that was once an important port located between Leigh and Southchurch. It was not until late in the 15th century that the name 'Southende' appears to have been used. At that time Prittlewell, Southchurch and Leigh were all well established, as were Hadleigh, Rochford and many of the smaller villages mentioned in this book.

By the middle of the 18th century it became fashionable to visit the seaside. It was thought that the sea air and water gave help to those with health problems. In 1758 The Ship Inn was built and by 1768 a private company realised that the coastal area to the south of Prittlewell might be an ideal place to develop as a bathing resort. This scheme failed, but as the century wore on, an increasing number of fashionable visitors did journey from London to Southend by horse-drawn coach or by the weekly packet boat.

More accommodation was needed, and plans were made to build a grand hotel at New Southe-End, with two terraces of fine houses. The area to be developed was at the top of what is now known as Pier Hill and the name was used to distinguish it from Old Southe-End. This was the area to the east that was expanding around the Ship Hotel. By that time a few bathing huts had been introduced for the use of visitors. The new hotel was finally ready for its opening in July 1793 by which time the High Street covered the track that once ran from Prittlewell to Milton. An article in 'Gentleman's Magazine' of 1794 predicted that Southend would soon be "all the rage".

It was the arrival of five year old Princess Charlotte and her mother Caroline, Princess of Wales, in 1801 that really made the growing town socially acceptable. The little princess was, at that time, second in line to the throne. Photographs of the well-preserved Royal Terrace, where these illustrious visitors stayed, can be seen in the following pages. Others came to enjoy the town, including Lady Hamilton (Lord Nelson's mistress), and Benjamin Disraeli. However, some people felt that Southend was too quiet!

In the early years of the 19th century the town flourished. A jetty for pleasure boats was built below the cliffs as early as 1802. Public rooms, a library and warm and cold sea water baths were opened. A steamboat service started in 1819. At this point Southend's well-known mud caused problems, as boats could not reach the shore at low tide. This led to the first wooden pier being started ten years later.

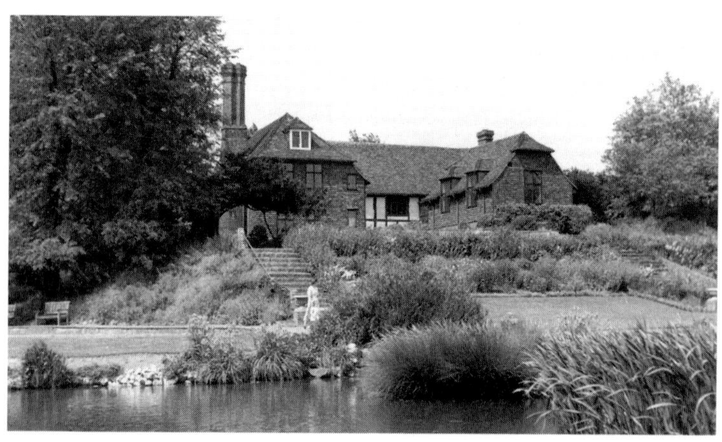

SOUTHEND, SOUTHCHURCH HALL, THE LAKE C1950 S155026

The pier was extended between 1834-35 and again in 1846, bringing its length to one and an eighth miles. This early pier was privately owned and poorly maintained. However, things improved after the Local Board bought it in 1875: re-building started and the new iron pier was opened to the public in 1889. The following year a single-track electric tramway began operating - the first pier railway in the country. Further extensions followed and by the early years of the 20th century Southend pier had become the symbol of the ever-growing town.

The pier played its part during the major wars of the 20th century. In the First World War sections came under Admiralty control and prisoners of war were taken along its length to waiting prison ships. At the commencement of the Second World War it was closed to the public and renamed HMS Leigh. It became a convoy control centre until its re-opening as a pleasure pier in 1945. Various disasters occurred over the years. Between 1898 and 1908 the pier sustained considerable damage after being hit three times by boats. Fire too has struck with disastrous results - in 1959 the beautiful Victorian Pavilion was totally destroyed. It was replaced by a 'modern' bowling alley. Fire struck again in July 1976 when the pier head met a spectacular end. Some of the remaining charred floor supports can still be seen. In 1995 yet another fire meant the end of the bowling alley. The Pier Museum, operated by knowledgeable volunteers belonging to the Southend Pier Museum Foundation, has an excellent display of memorabilia and information on the history of this unique structure.

It was the coming of the railway in 1856 that completely changed the character of the town. Visitors no longer had to make a dangerous sea trip or endure a long and uncomfortable journey by horse-drawn carriage. They could reach the town easily, stay for the day, and return home at night. Southend was close enough to the east end of London to make such trip a real possibility. The time of the day-tripper had arrived.

As the town flourished moves were made to gain the status of municipal borough and Queen Victoria signed the Charter of Incorporation in 1892. Great celebrations followed the reading of the Charter to a large crowd gathered at the top of Pier Hill. At this point the town was officially named Southend-on-Sea. Expansion continued and the new borough began swallowing up some of its much older neighbours. Westcliff, Chalkwell and Prittlewell had all became part of the town in 1877, and Southchurch was incorporated in 1897. Leigh-on-Sea became a part of the borough in 1913, with Eastwood and Shoebury joining in 1933. New housing estates were built for the ever-growing population. County Borough status was achieved in 1914.

Often called 'London's Playground', Southend has long been famous for its Golden Mile, Illuminations, Carnival and The Kursaal, noted for its distinctive dome. The Kursaal was opened to the public in 1901 and went on to become one of the best-known amusement centres in the country. The park finally closed in 1974. Much of the site is now used for housing, although the dome remains. The Golden Mile became a centre for amusement arcades, cafes and public houses. The annual Carnival was started in 1926 to raise money for the new Southend General Hospital and it has remained a popular event ever since.

Between the Wars the town flourished and, following the end of the Second World War, there was a brief a return to the golden age of the seaside. However, all that was about to change, due to the growing demand for a more sophisticated type of holiday.

1935 saw the opening of the Municipal Airport, built on the site of a First World War aerodrome that was used again during the Second World War. In many ways it was the growth of air travel that led to the decline of the seaside town; once it became easy to reach countries with more settled climates, towns like Southend became less attractive.

Many fine reminders of the Victorian and Edwardian ages were lost during the building boom of the 1960s and 70s. Victoria Circus was re-developed and a large shopping centre replaced Garons and The Talza Arcade. The High Street was pedestrianised and Supa-Save, built on the site of the Strand Cinema, was a pioneer of supermarket development. The beautiful bandstand, so *popular with the Edwardians, was removed and a plain stage took its place. Ideas have, however, now gone full circle and a bandstand once again stands on the top of the cliffs.*

The Southend area is fortunate in having some superb parks. Parts of the old Prittlewell Priory still stand and are open to the public. In 1920 R A Jones, a prominent local jeweller and benefactor of the town, gave this delightful property to the borough. With its ancient fishponds and magnificent trees and gardens it is well worth a visit. The grounds of Chalkwell Hall became a park noted for its rose gardens. The smaller gardens around Leigh Library form a peaceful haven close to the busy centre of the town. Southchurch Hall is now a museum, but the moat and gardens take the visitor back to the time when this was an impressive manor house. The Churchill Gardens too, although small, are much loved by those working in the large civic buildings found in Victoria Avenue.

By the 1980s the old-style seaside town had declined in popularity. Trippers still came into Southend by train, coach and car, but the commercial centre of the town had moved to Victoria Avenue. Some industry developed in the area but the town needed new attractions at its 'south end'. An annual Air Show has now become popular. The Royals Shopping Centre, located at the top of Pier Hill, is well established, although the construction of this complex necessitated the demolition of many old buildings. A large aquarium is sited near the pier and Adventure Island is a must for children.

Fortunately we still have photographic records of earlier times and, within these pages, you will find some of those reminders to take you on a journey down memory lane.

For our exploration of Southend, we will approach from the west along the A13, stopping off at various towns and villages along the way. We will visit the town itself, then pause for a while in some of the towns and villages to the north, before reaching the A127 to return in the London direction.

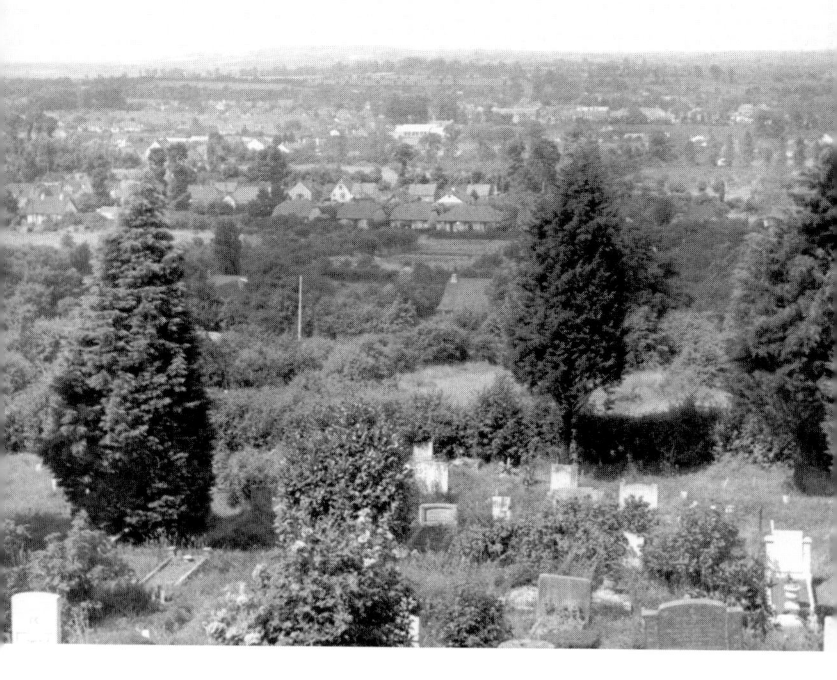

This churchyard stands at the top of Thundersley Church Road, well removed from the bustle of the town below. The church of St Peter, standing further up the hill, has a nave and aisles dating from the early 13th century. The town name is believed to have come from the pagan worship of Thunor.

THUNDERSLEY

THE VIEW FROM THE CHURCHYARD   c1955 / T113027

Canvey Island was a popular holiday resort in the 1950s. Well-ordered rows of caravans are ready to welcome summer visitors. A complex of administrative buildings can also be seen. This photograph clearly illustrates the flatness of much of the reclaimed land that forms the island and which the sea attempted to reclaim in the devastating floods of 1953.

CANVEY ISLAND

THORNEY BAY BEACH CAMP c1955 / C237304

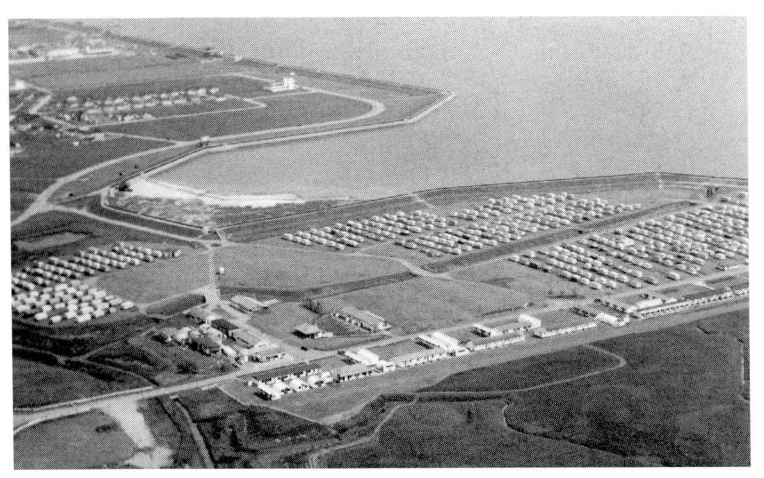

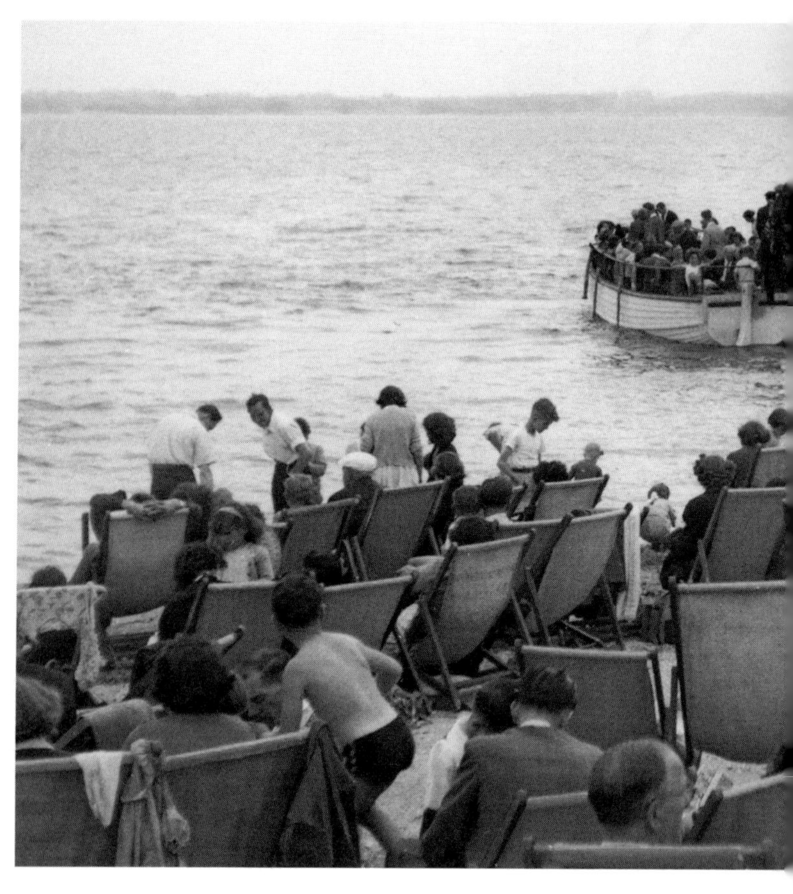

CANVEY ISLAND

A BEACH SCENE   c1955 / C237065

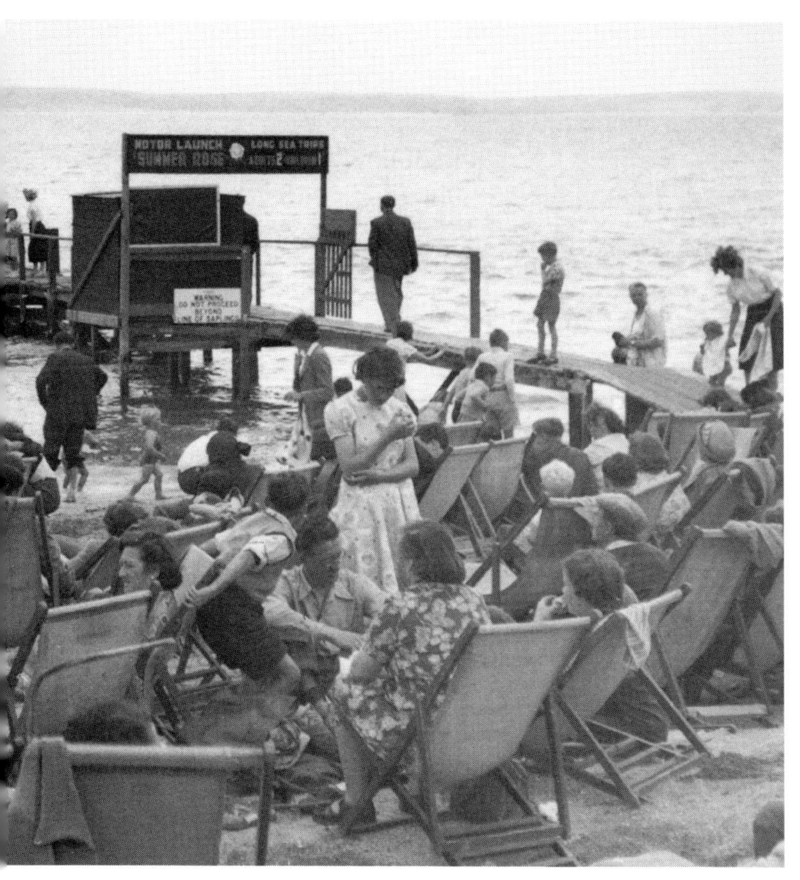

There is little room for making sand-pies on this crowded beach. Deck-chairs occupy all the available space as would-be sailors await their turn to board the motor launch 'Summer Rose'. Adults paid 2 shillings and children 1 shilling for what is described as 'a long sea trip'.

Another view of the beach at Canvey Island shows children busily playing around the many deckchairs. Most of the older holidaymakers are well wrapped up against the cold. Rather battered breakwaters give some protection from erosion to the sand and shingle beach.

CANVEY ISLAND

SHELL BEACH   C1955 / C237005

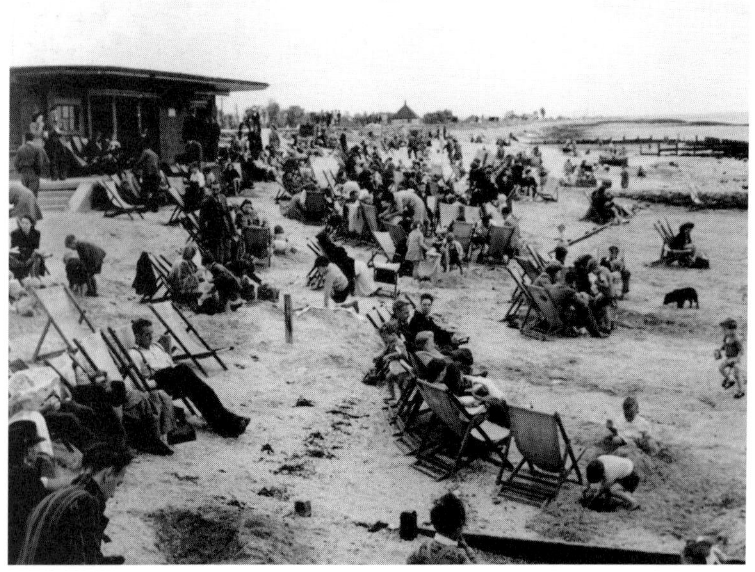

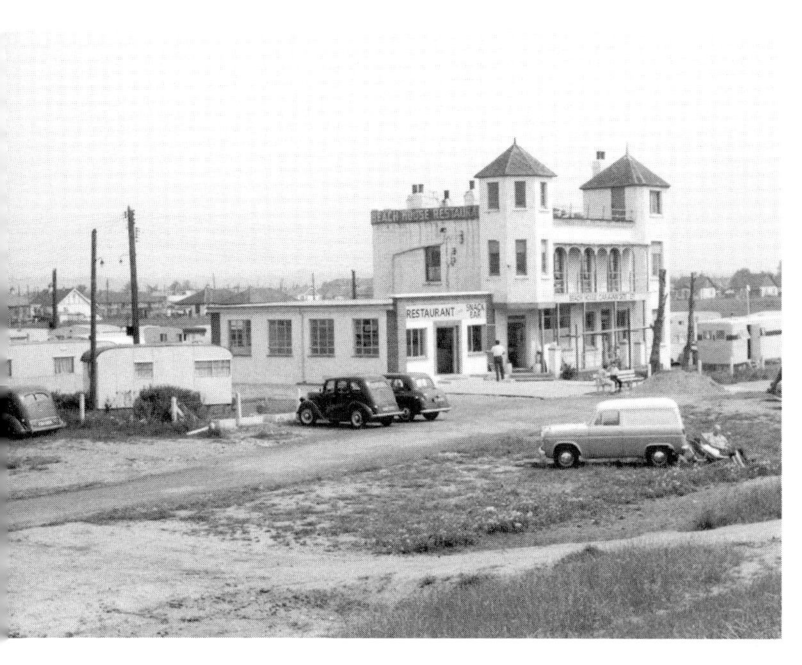

The flat nature of the surrounding countryside is again shown in this photograph. Caravans nestle close to the large Beach House Café. This is an interesting building, with its two end towers and decorative façade. It seems too impressive for these surroundings.

CANVEY ISLAND

THE BEACH HOUSE CAFÉ   C1955 / C237122

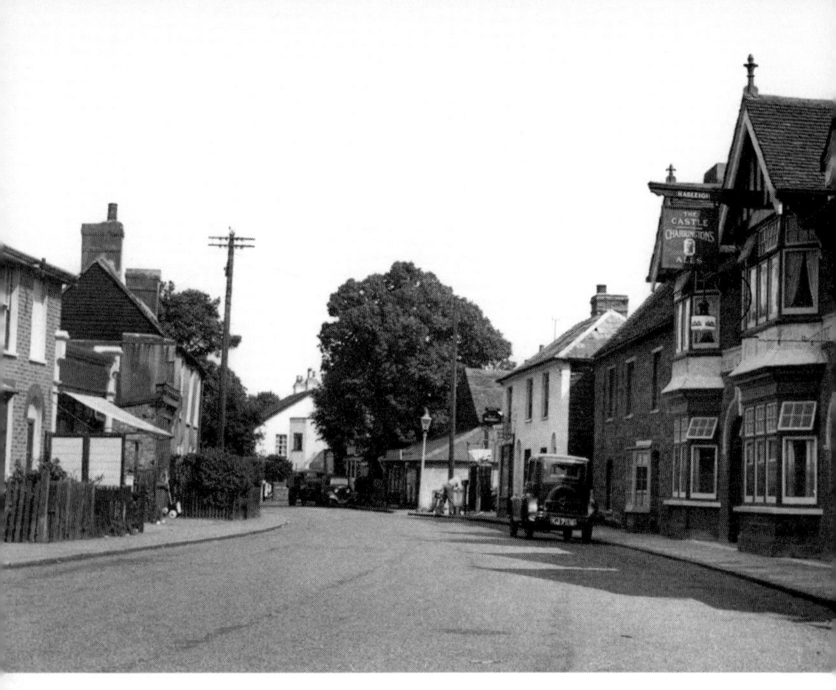

The Castle Hotel, with its gabled roof and solid appearance, takes its name from Hadleigh Castle. Although this photograph shows the High Street, it lacks the bustle we see today. A small garage is tucked in next to a café on the right, whilst on the left brick-built houses with fenced gardens stand alongside small shops protected by awnings.

HADLEIGH

THE HIGH STREET   C1950 / H167010

This scene again shows The Castle Hotel, but from the west. In the intervening years since H167010 (opposite page) was taken, the Esso Garage has obviously expanded, although the cottages and shops on the right are little changed. Cars have become sleeker, but note the price of the one shown on the forecourt - a snip at £226! The street lamp in this picture is less decorative than the one in the earlier view.

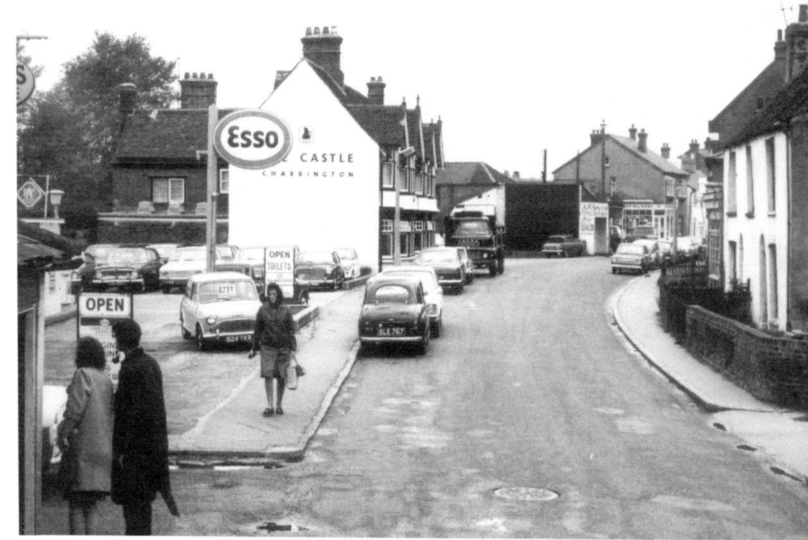

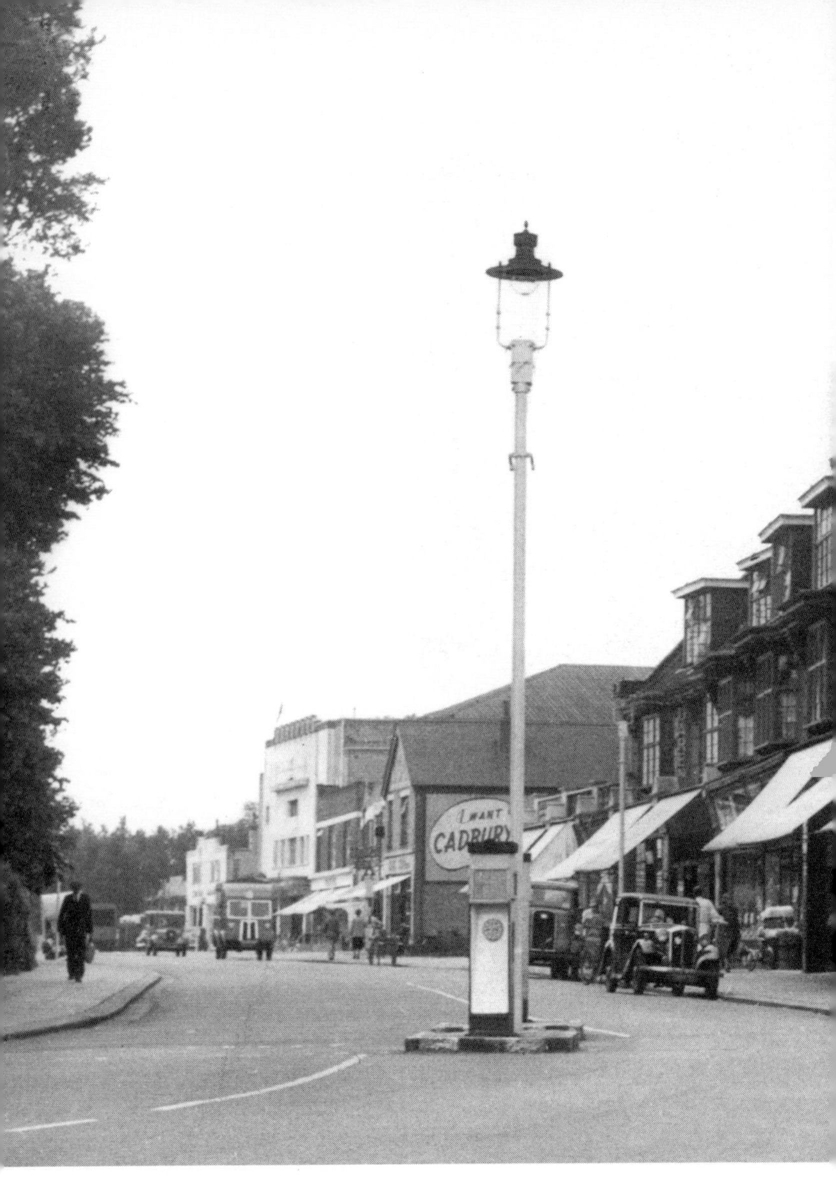

I WANT
CADBURY'S

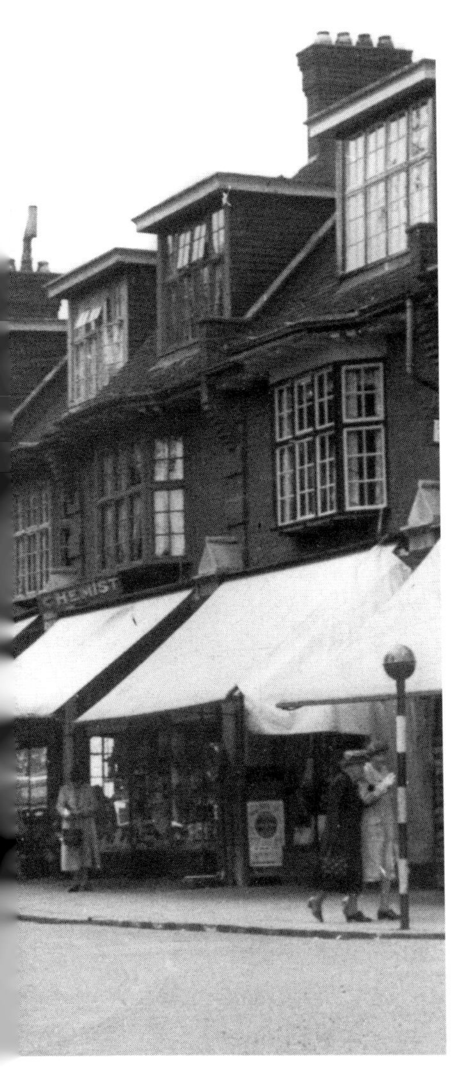

This busy row of shops, with living accommodation above, faces the grounds of the ancient church of St James the Less, dating from the 12th century. Plain shop walls could be used to advertise products such as Cadbury's. The Kingsway Cinema was a popular place of entertainment in the area.

HADLEIGH

CENTRAL PARADE

c1950 / H167003

Hubert de Burgh was granted a licence in 1230 for the construction of the castle. However, it was completely re-built in the time of Edward III. Little now remains of the massive structure that once stood on this site, although two of the towers may still be seen. A number of Plantagenet kings and their wives were associated with the castle. The building was immortalised by the artist John Constable.

HADLEIGH

THE CASTLE   C1955 / H167008

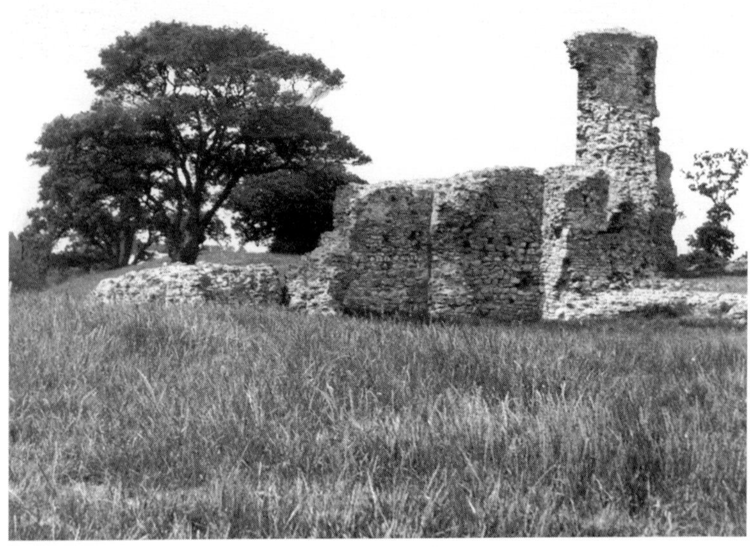

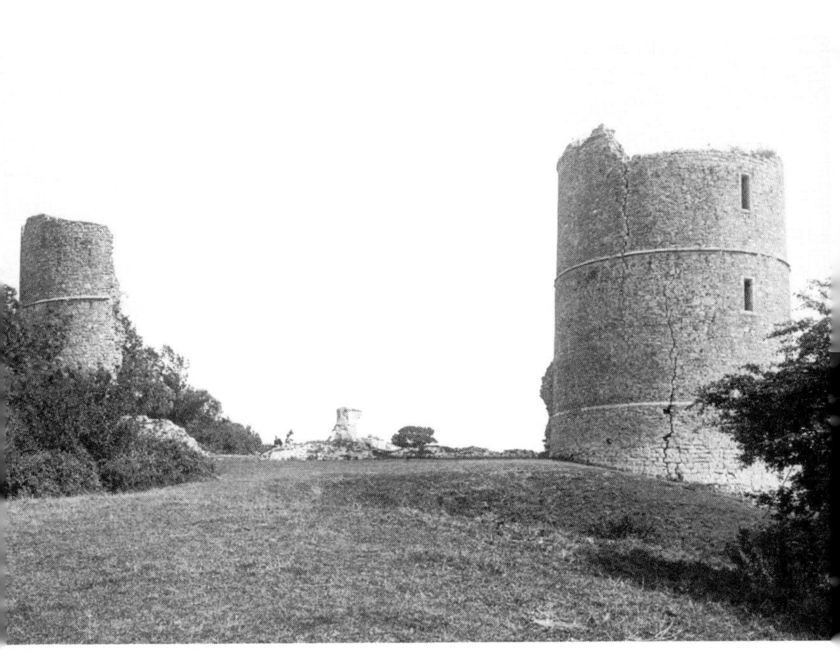

The castle had two main towers and a further tower guarding the entrance on the north side. There was no keep. Kentish Ragstone was brought across the River Thames for the construction. Here we see two of those towers, situated at the east end of the site. Deep cracks have appeared in the better-preserved tower.

HADLEIGH

THE CASTLE 1891 / 29071

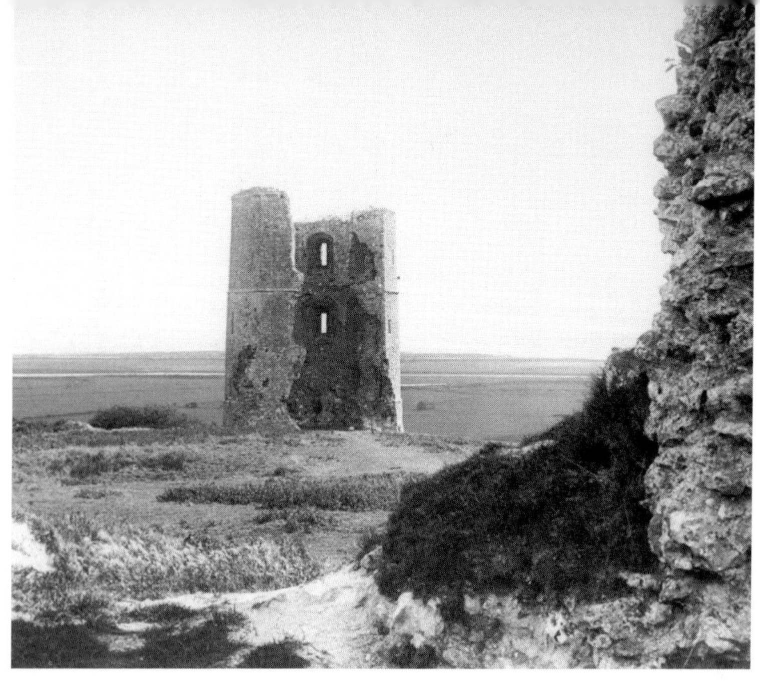

This view of the towers is taken from inside the ruins. The castle stands on high ground with excellent views over the widening river. The building fell into disrepair, especially after Lord Rich bought it in 1551. Much of the stone was used in other buildings in the area.

HADLEIGH

THE CASTLE   1891 / 29070

HADLEIGH

Looking across the fields towards the ruins of the castle it is apparent how little remains of the original building. There are excellent walks in the area. The ruins are now cared for by English Heritage.

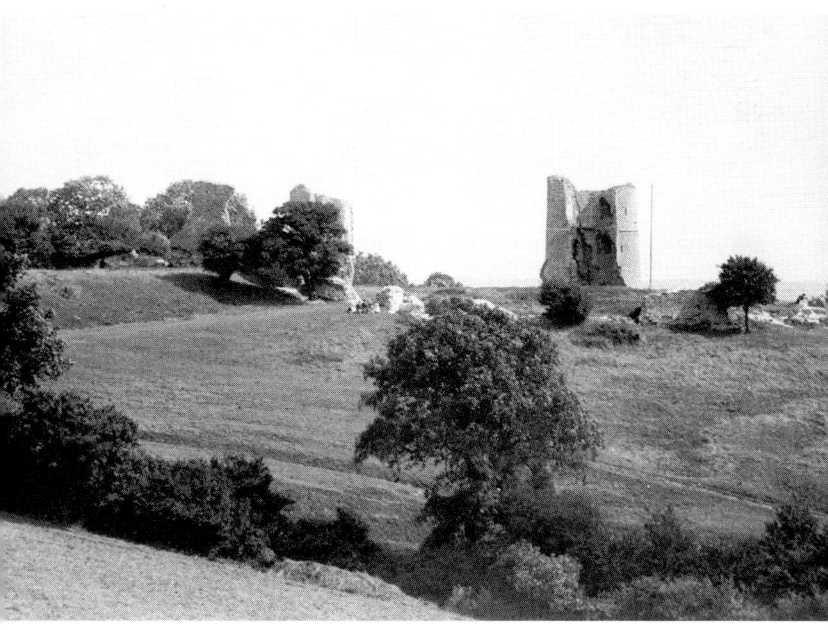

LEIGH-ON-SEA

FROM THE WEST   1891 / 29065

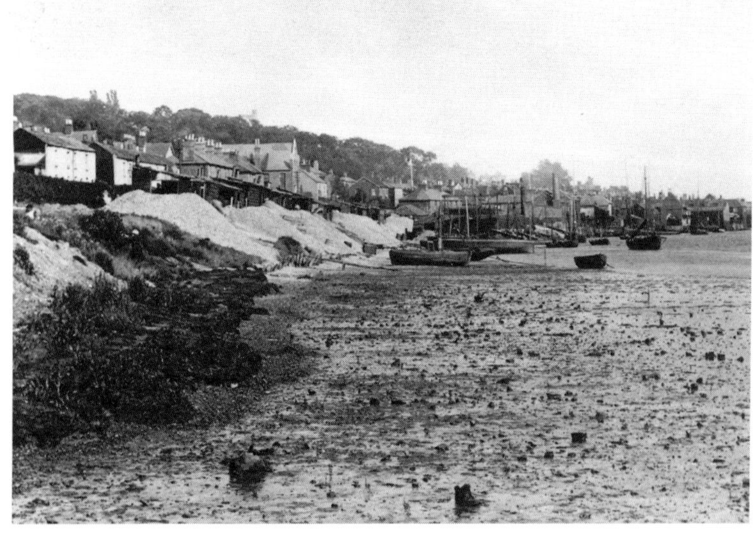

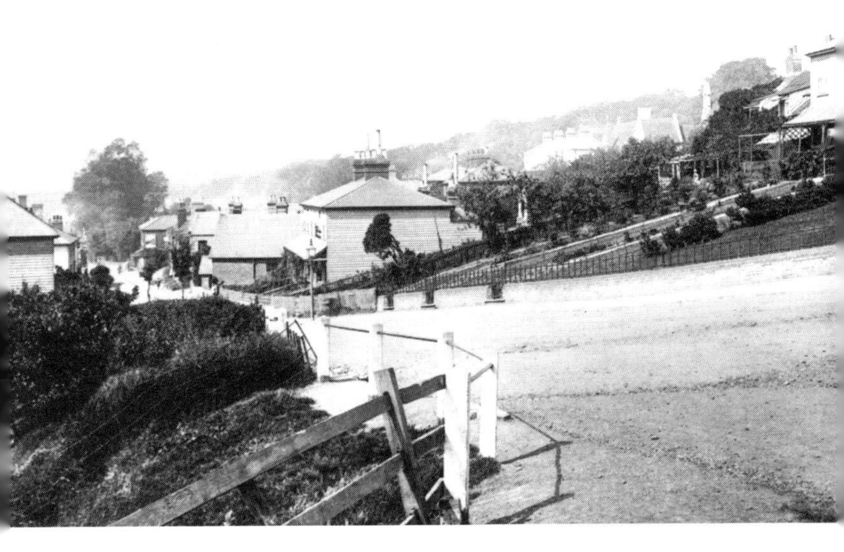

Leigh is noted for its weatherboard cottages. Essex lacks natural rock so skills in the use of wood and brick-making have been well developed over the centuries. Attractive wrought iron fencing surrounds the long gardens on the right.

LEIGH-ON-SEA
FROM THE WEST 1891 / 29066

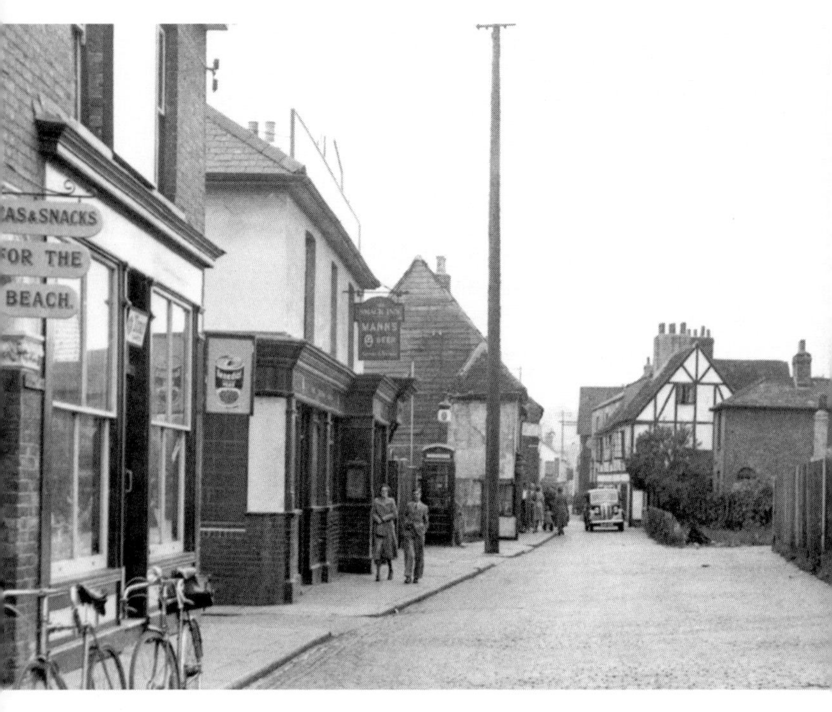

This is part of Old Leigh, with the railway on the right and the sea behind the buildings on the left. The main shopping centre has moved up the hill to Leigh Broadway but this High Street is still popular with its cafes, public houses and antiques shops. There is a quaint, old-world feel to this part of the town. At one time many of these buildings were in danger of demolition to make way for a new road. Fortunately the scheme was abandoned.

LEIGH-ON-SEA
HIGH STREET c1950 / L30024

LEIGH-ON-SEA

THE CLIFF SHELTER   C1955 / L30039

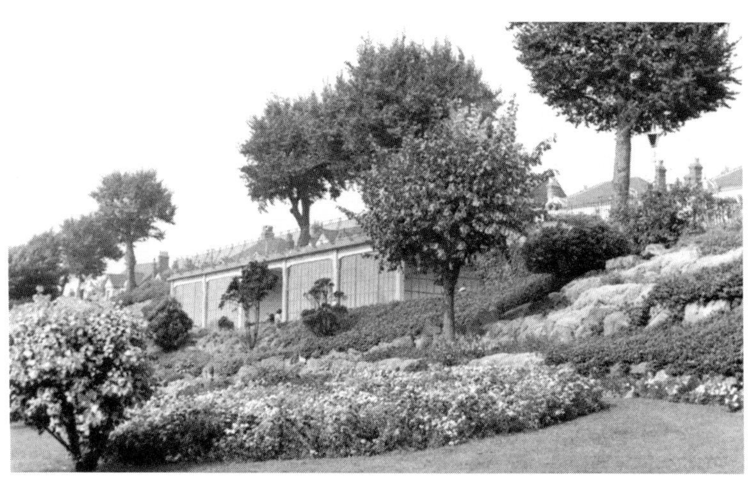

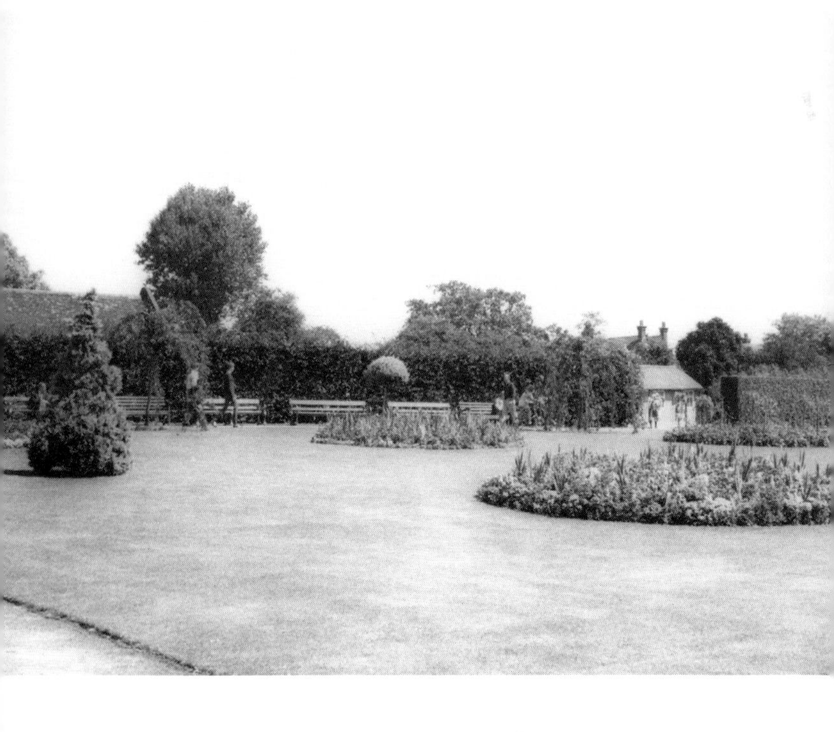

Chalkwell Park was formed from the grounds surrounding Chalkwell Hall. The Council purchased this land in 1901. It became noted for its rose gardens and as the popular centre for the annual Carnival funfair. The picture shows some of the well-kept flower beds.

SOUTHEND

CHALKWELL PARK   C1960 / S155136

SOUTHEND

WESTCLIFF PARADE   1898 / 41386

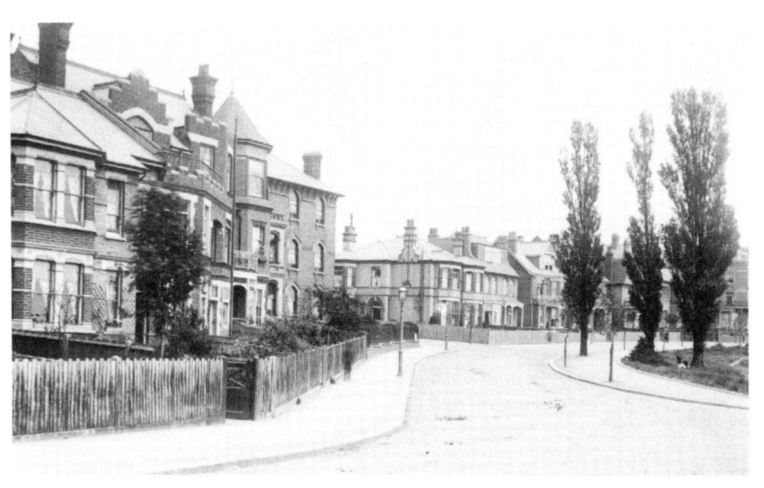

SOUTHEND

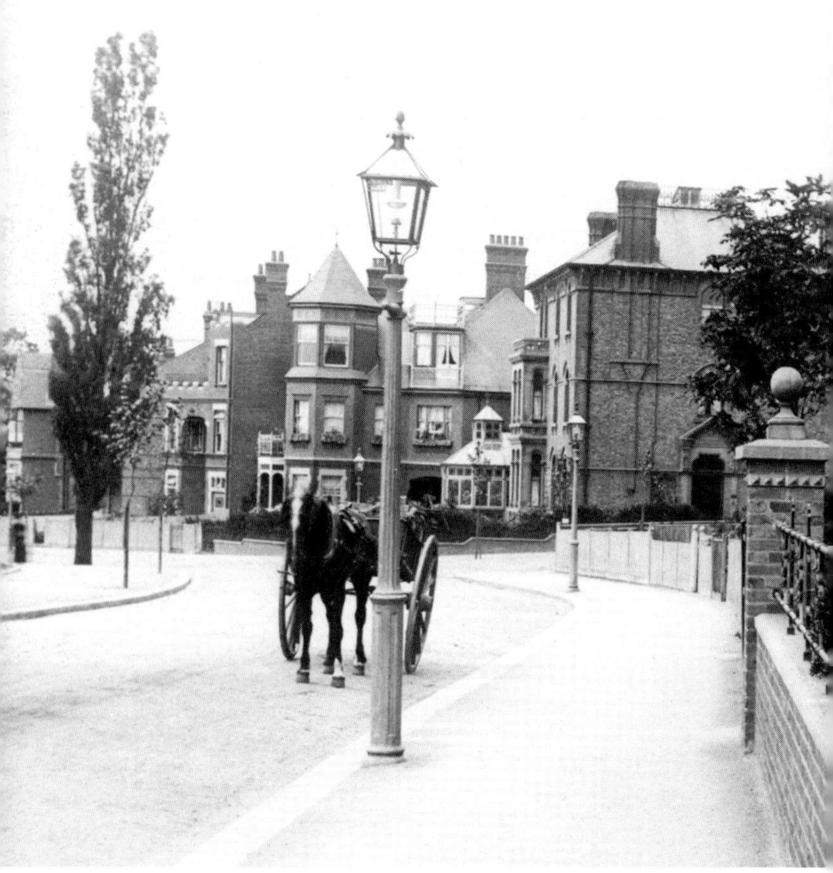

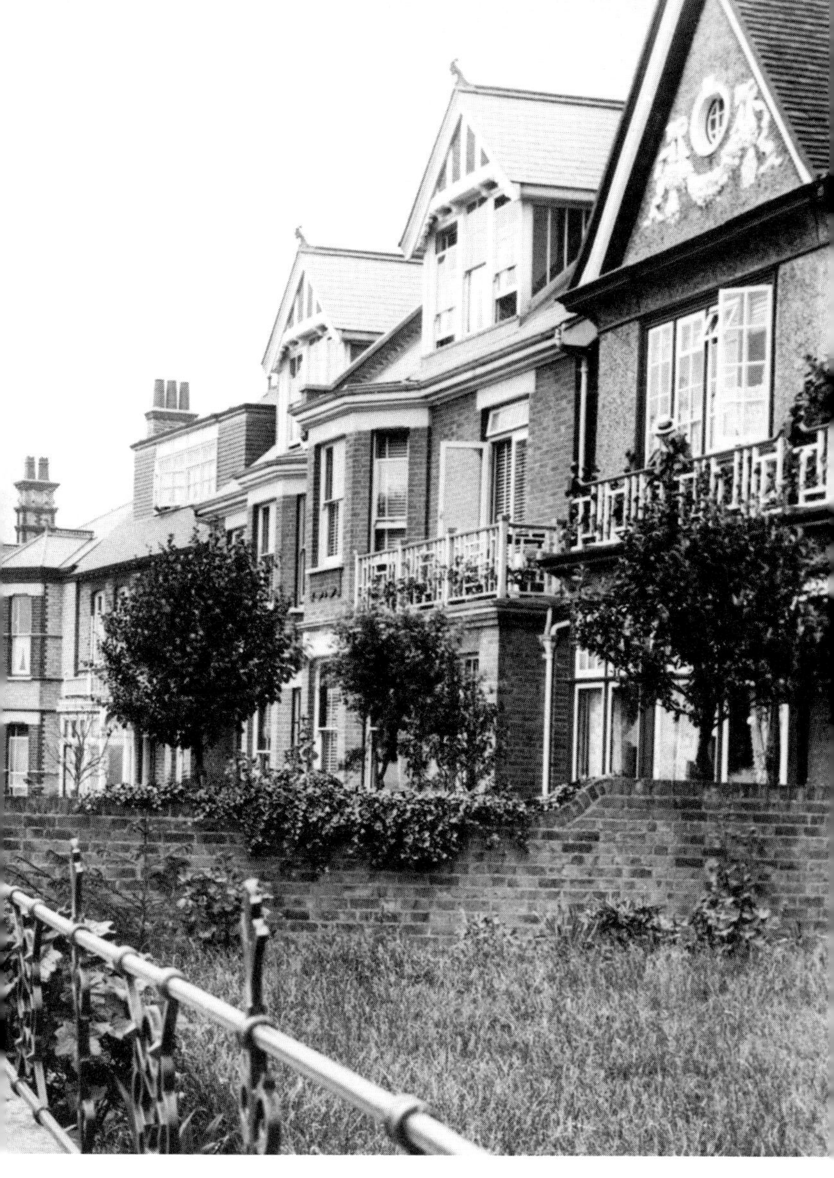

SOUTHEND

MARINE GARDENS   c1950 / S155034

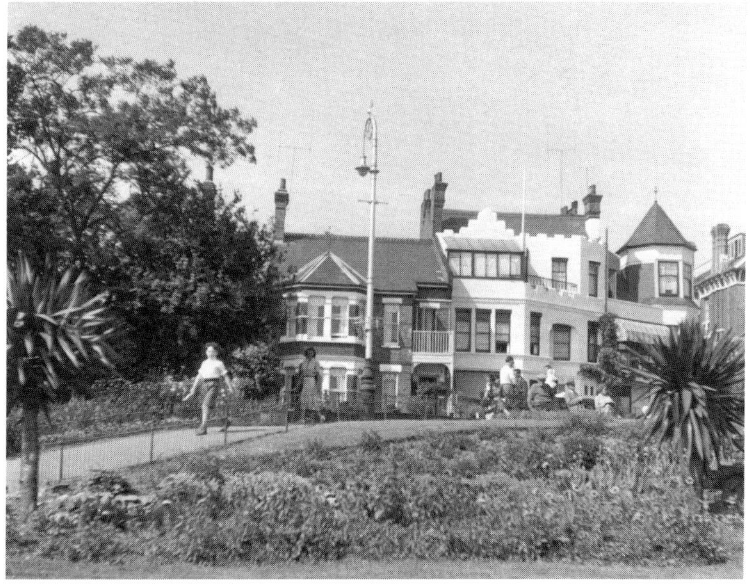

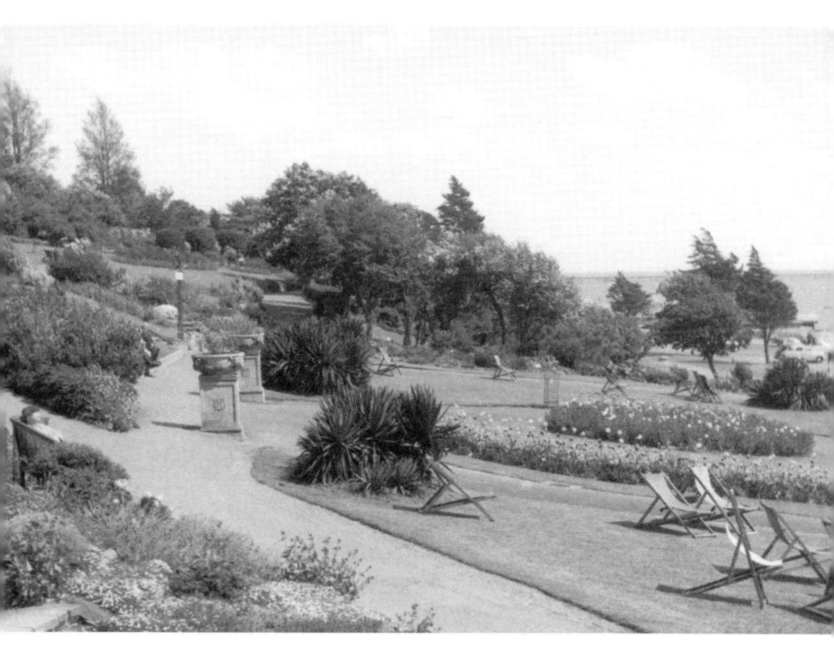

Here we see some of the gardens to the west of the main town, much enjoyed by residents and visitors. The land slopes more gently than in the Shrubbery area.

SOUTHEND

THE UNDERCLIFF GARDENS   C1955 / S155053

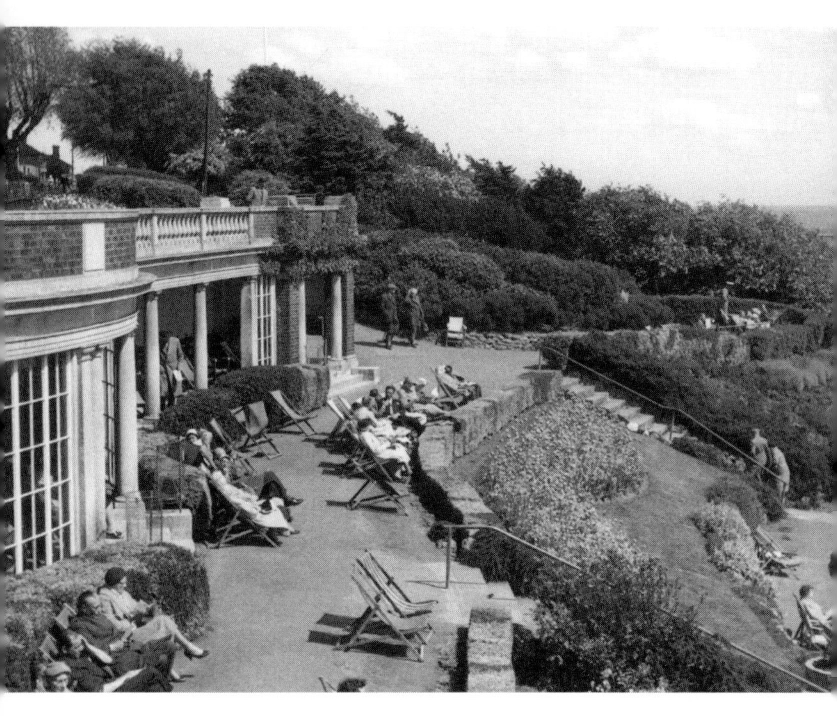

The Cliffs Shelter, shown here, was fitted with Vita-Glass. This, it was claimed, gave the benefit of the health-giving rays of the sun to those sitting behind its protection. Walkers could stand on the roof of the shelter to enjoy the view. None of this glass remains in place.

SOUTHEND

THE UNDERCLIFF GARDENS   C1955 / S155056

SOUTHEND

WESTCLIFF PARADE   C1955 / S155058

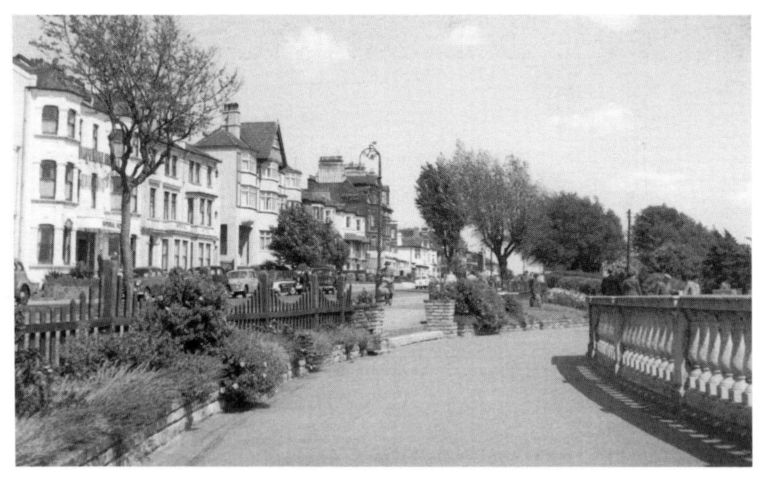

37

The West Cliff was one of the hotels in the Westcliff area and was always a popular venue for wedding receptions. Overlooking the Cliff Gardens, many of its rooms had excellent sea views. It underwent extensive renovation in the 1980s.

SOUTHEND

WESTCLIFF c1960 / S155096

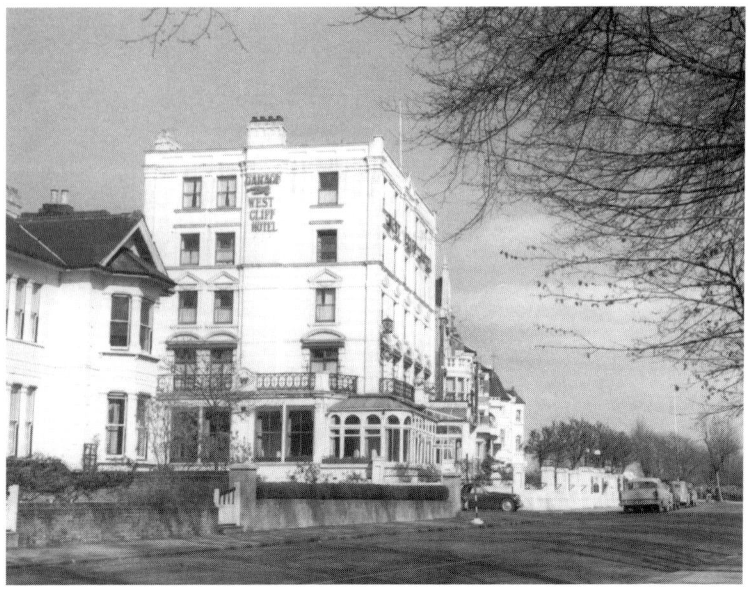

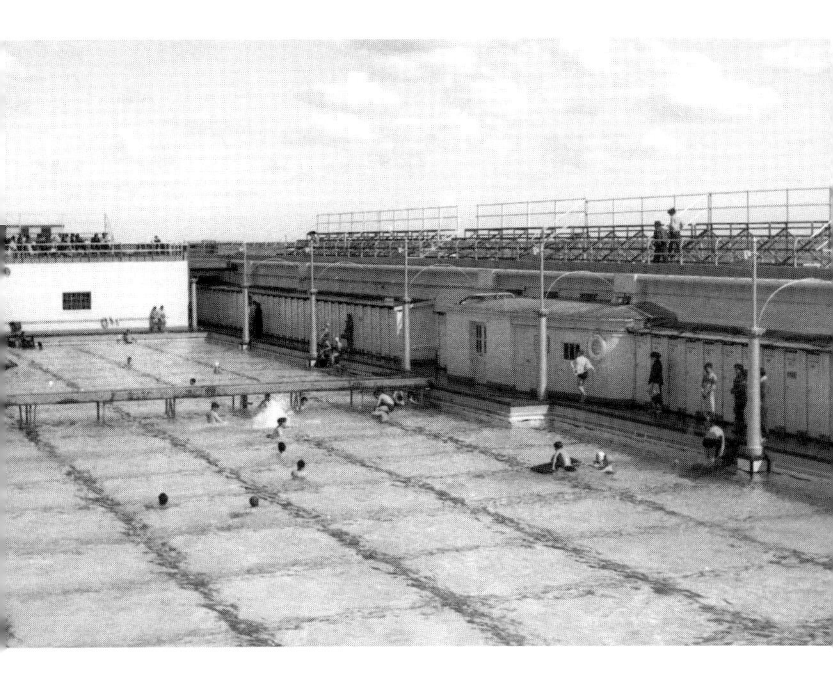

The Southend Corporation Swimming Bath on Western Esplanade was a popular feature of the town. 300ft x 75ft, it boasted a high diving board, platforms, chutes and springboards. Dressing cubicles can be seen behind those standing on the side. Many seats were provided for spectators and there was a terrace for sunbathing.

SOUTHEND
WESTCLIFF POOL C1955 / S155047

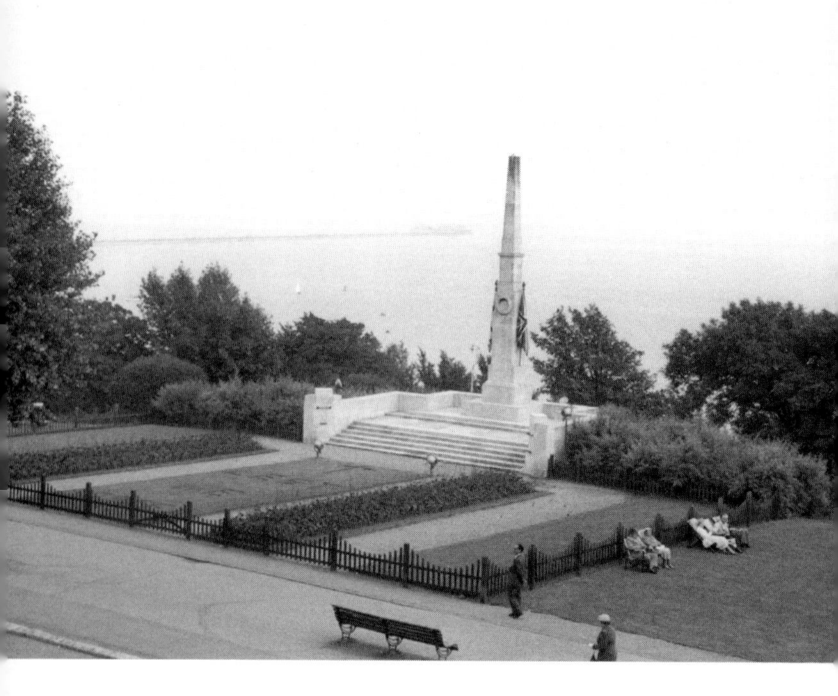

The impressive War Memorial stands to the west of the bandstand on high ground overlooking the sea. Commemorating those lost in the wars of the 20th century, it is used for the annual Remembrance Day Service. The pier can be seen in the background.

SOUTHEND

THE WAR MEMORIAL   C1955 / S155042

SOUTHEND

WESTCLIFF   C1955 / S155043

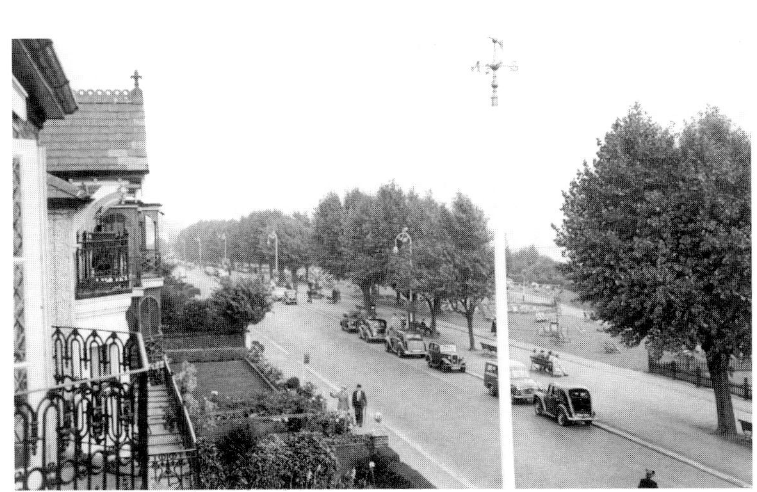

This ornate cast-iron bandstand dates from 1909 when it replaced an earlier wooden structure. The open-air concerts held here were very popular and some shelter was provided. Note the array of chimney pots on the houses behind the shelters.

SOUTHEND
THE BAND STAND   C1950 / S155032

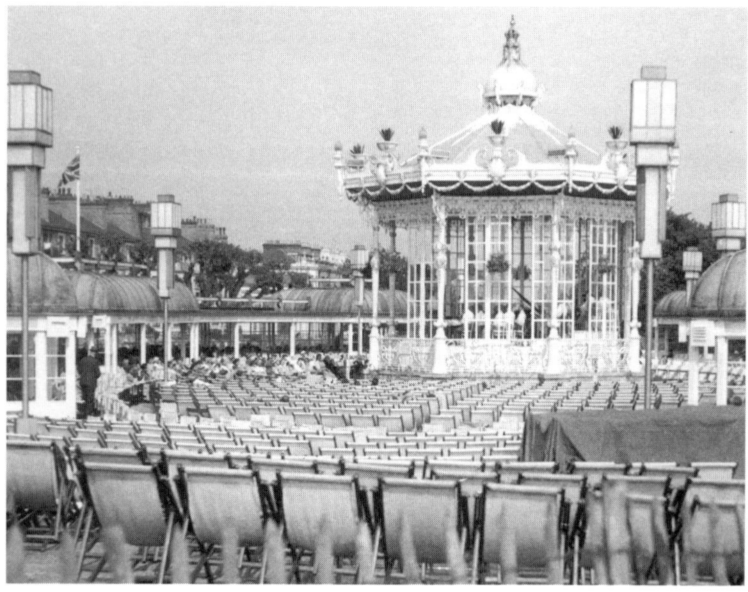

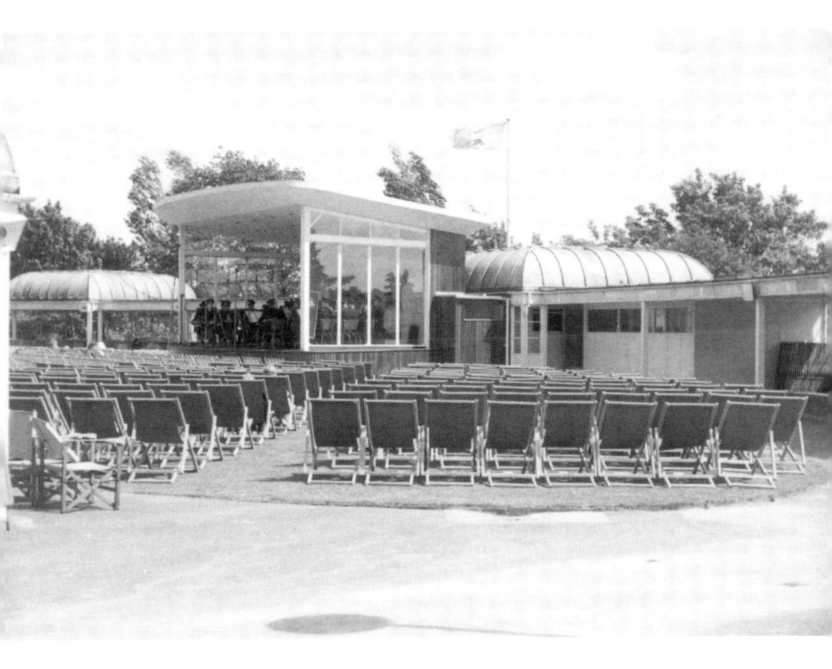

This plain stage replaced the earlier Edwardian bandstand. Deck chairs still provided the main form of seating. The shelters remain unchanged. From the position of the flag this appears to be a windy day - possibly accounting for the small size of the audience.

SOUTHEND

WESTCLIFF PARADE BAND STAGE   C1955 / S155059

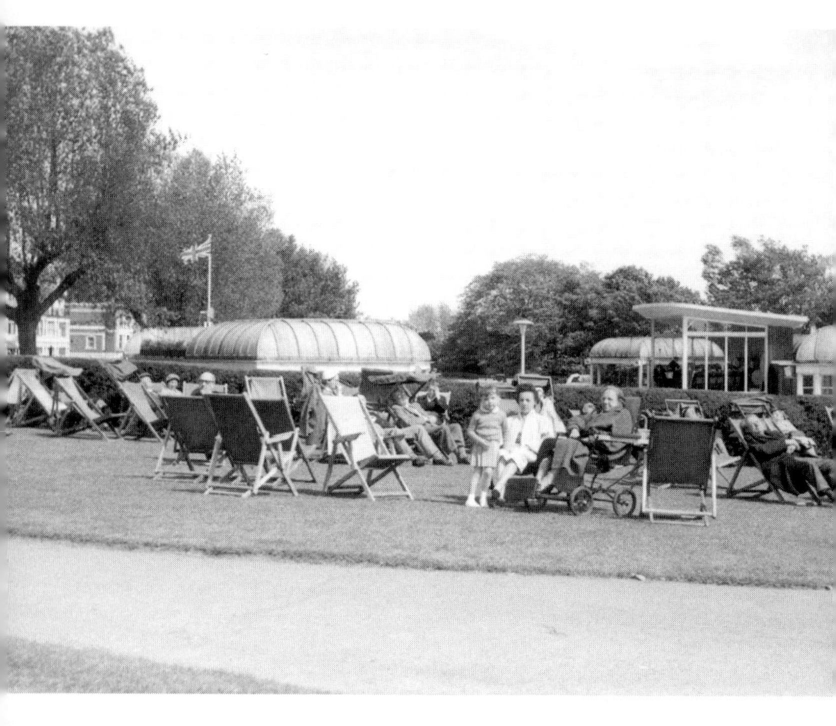

Well wrapped up against the wind, holiday-makers still managed to enjoy the sunshine and music close to the band stage, using the grass verges for their deck chairs. A band can be seen performing in the background.

SOUTHEND
WESTCLIFF PARADE BAND STAGE   C1955 / S155061

Close to the band stage and above the tree-covered cliffs are wide expanses of grass, ideal for picnics. The lady on the right looks as if she is auditioning for 'The Sound of Music', but perhaps she has been inspired by the playing of the band.

SOUTHEND

THE WESTCLIFF GARDENS   c1955 / S155064

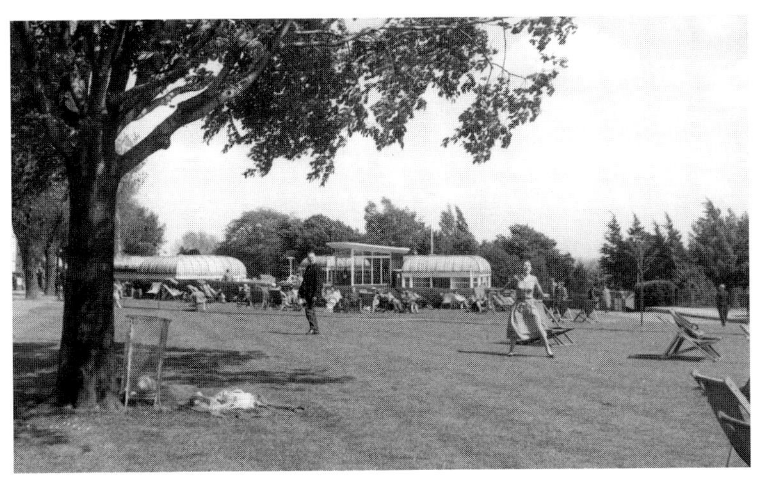

SOUTHEND

WESTCLIFF PARADE   c1955 / S155066

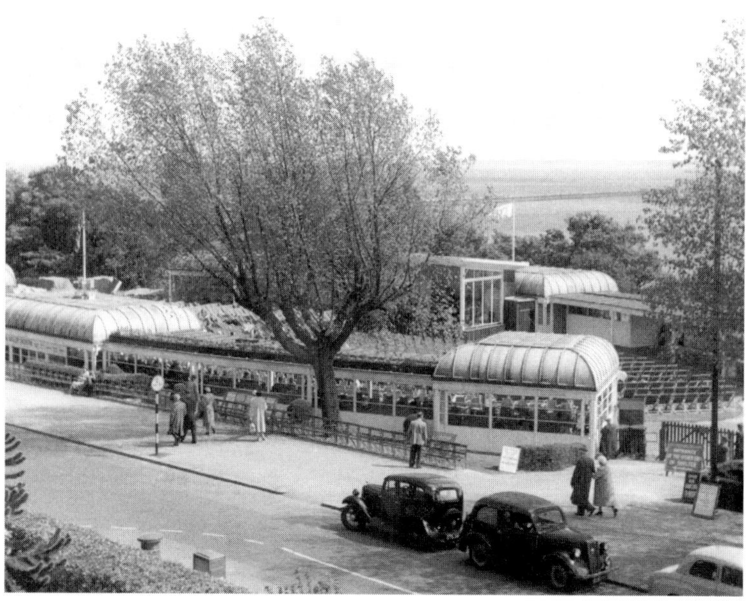

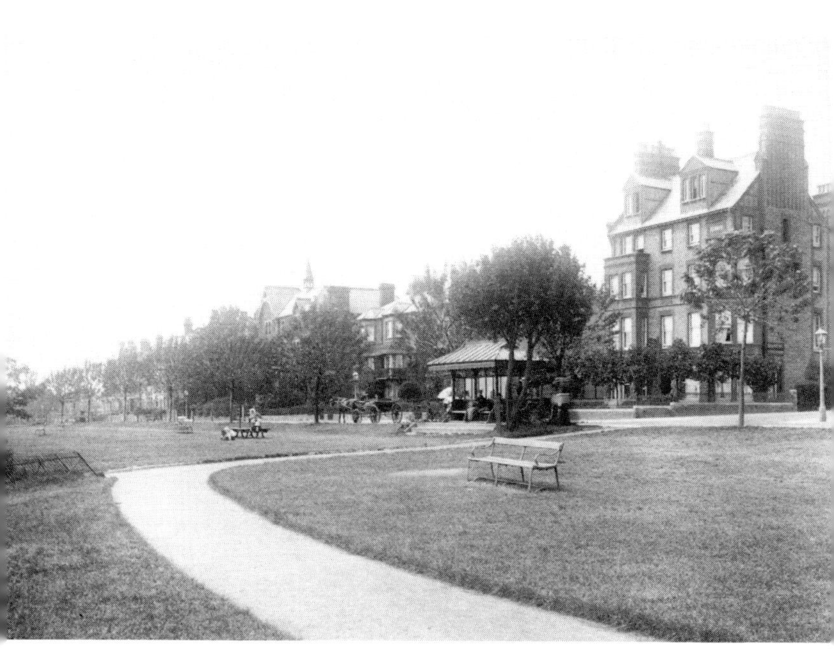

Moving closer to the main town of Southend-on-Sea, The Westward Ho! Boarding Establishment dominates this scene. It went on to become one of the premier hotels of the town. Now the name is used by a new tower block which stands on the site. A horse-drawn carriage can be seen close to the shelter, the only form of transport in sight.

SOUTHEND

ON THE CLIFFS   1898 / 41385

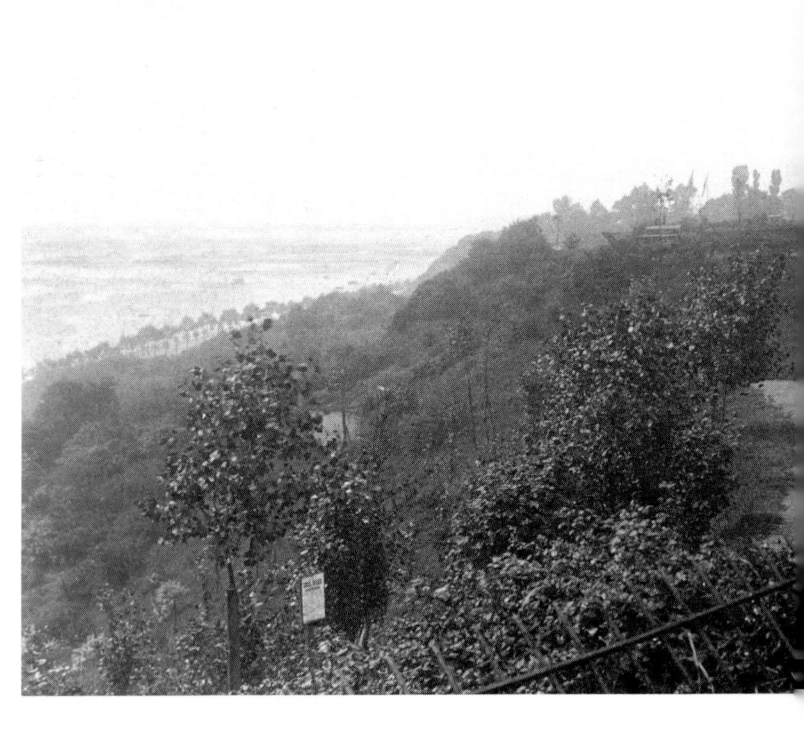

SOUTHEND

ON THE CLIFFS   1891 / 29048

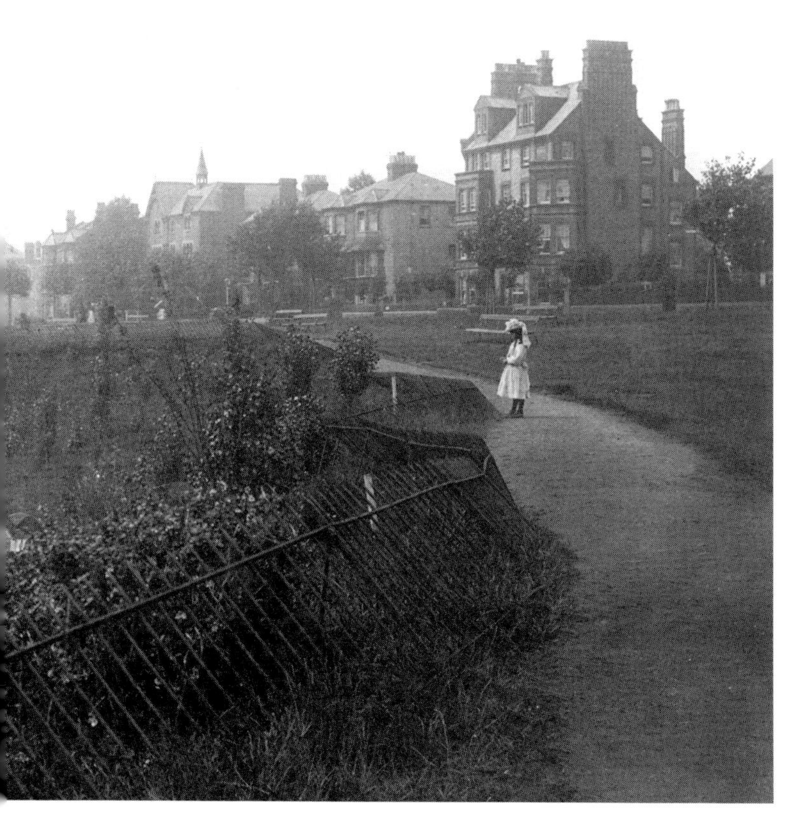

The clay cliffs at Southend have always been prone to slipping. Frequently, over the years, notices have been erected closing the threatened areas. Here we see railings lying at a very strange angle, probably as a result of this problem. The little girl, in her large hat, may have looked smart, but such clothes were certainly not designed for play.

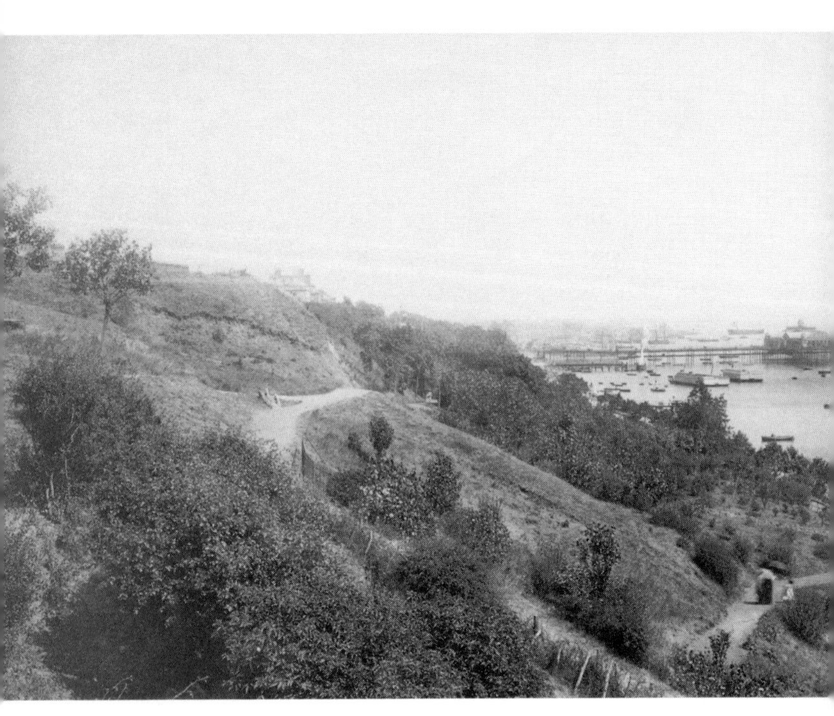

Although there are well-defined paths, the cliff gardens have yet to be laid out in a formal way. The pier and Pavilion can be seen on the right with many boats close by. A walker on the right is protected from the weather by an umbrella or sunshade.

SOUTHEND

FROM THE CLIFFS   1895 / 35654

SOUTHEND

TERRACES WESTCLIFF   1898 / 40913

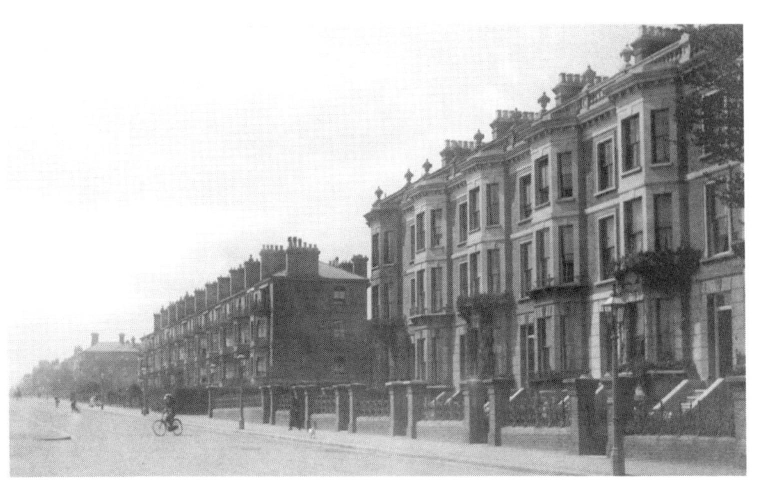

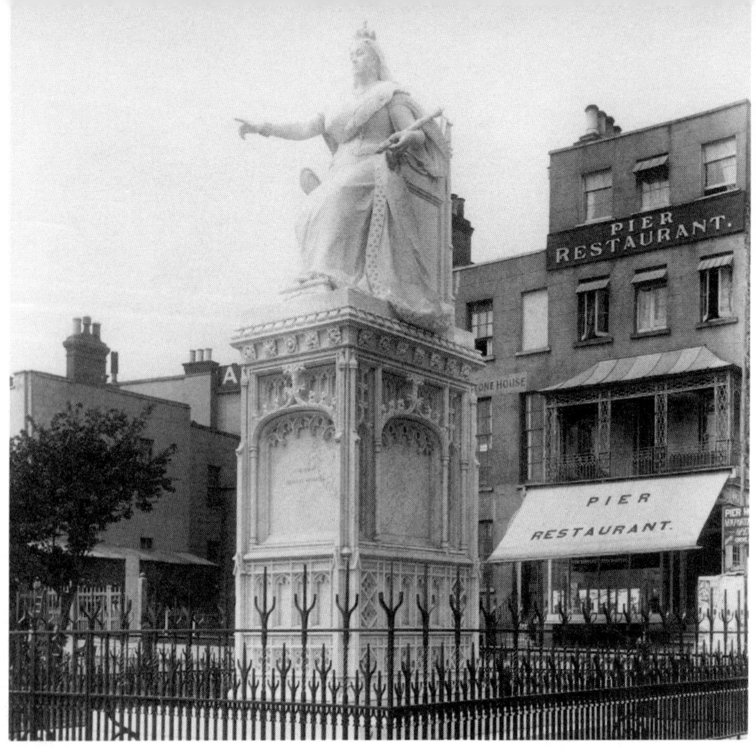

Queen Victoria's Diamond Jubilee was celebrated in Southend with the erection of this statue at the top of Pier Hill. Well protected by railings, the queen points regally out to sea. In later years the statue suffered from vandalism and has now been moved further to the west, near the bandstand.

SOUTHEND

QUEEN'S STATUE   1898 / 41388

ROYAL TERRACE   1891 / 29061

Railings and decorative wrought iron work were both popular at this time. Royal Terrace stretches away towards the High Street. On the right are The Shrubbery Gardens. St John's Church can be seen in the distance.

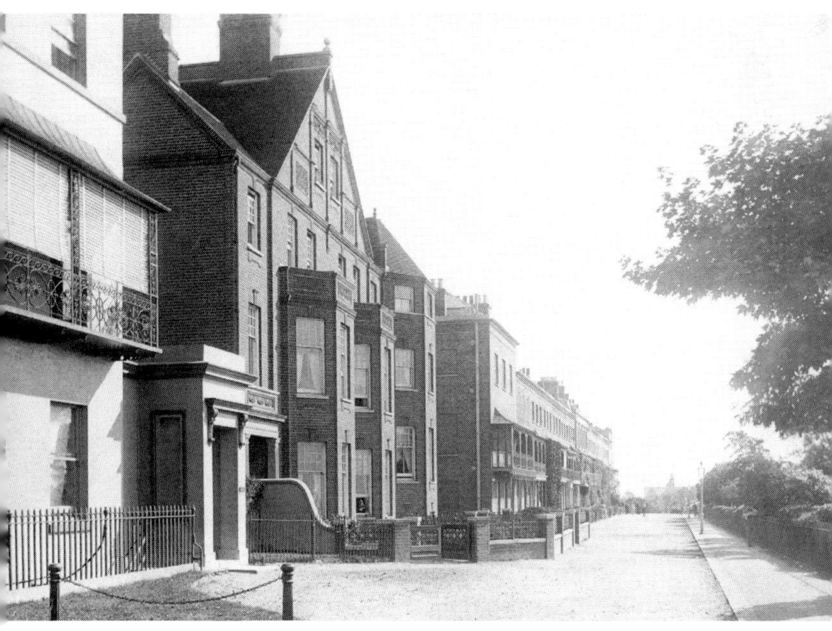

Moving away from the seaside, via Southend High Street, the Civic Centre is to be found in Victoria Avenue. Where once Prittlewell Church dominated the skyline now this massive Civic Centre building has taken over. Steel and glass were used in the construction of these offices, opened by the Queen Mother in 1967. The complex includes the Town Hall, Law Courts, Police Headquarters and the Technical College, all built close to the Civic Square. Victoria Avenue can be seen on the left.

SOUTHEND

THE CIVIC CENTRE   c1960 / S155191

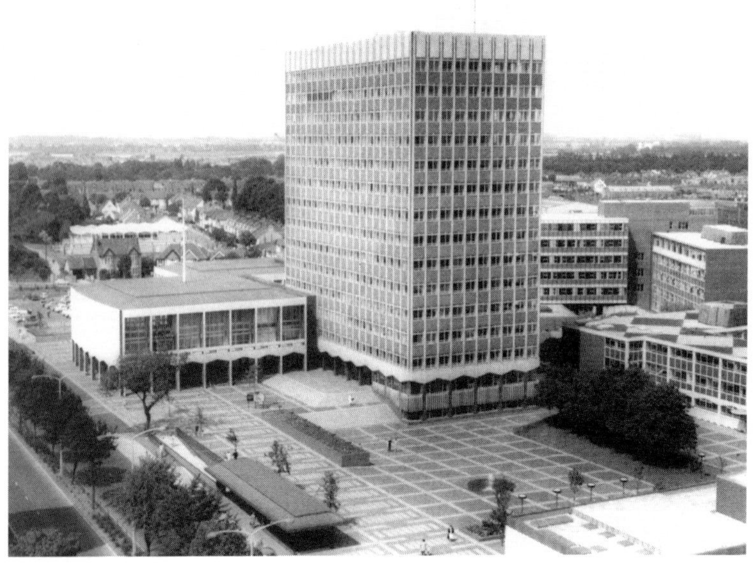

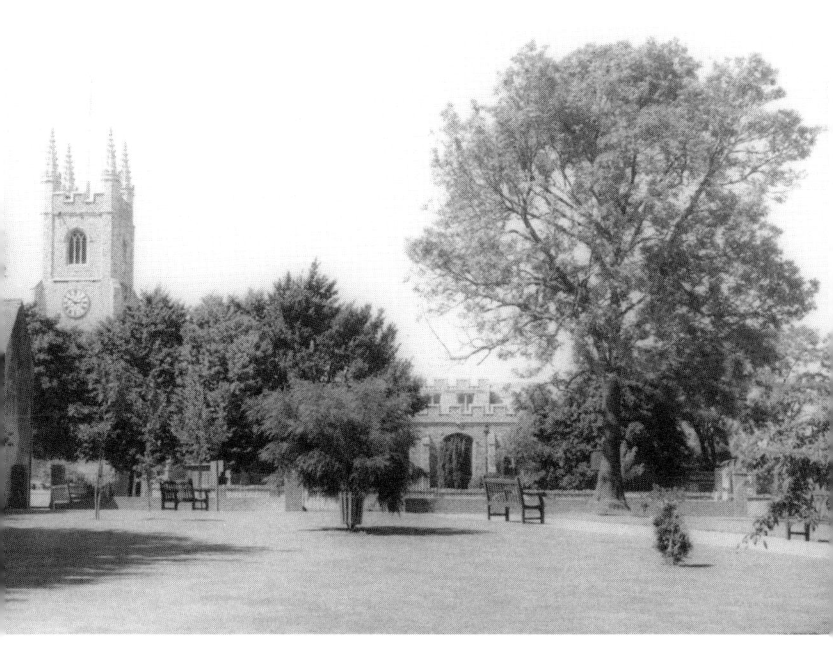

This beautiful sunken garden has been created in a disused
gravel pit. Following the death of the owner, the site was
acquired by the town and first opened to the public in 1960.
Dedicated to the memory of Sir Winston Churchill, this
long, narrow garden is a delight to visit in spring when the
high banks are a mass of flowers. In the background
Prittlewell Church can be seen.

SOUTHEND

CHURCHILL GARDENS   c1960 / S155148

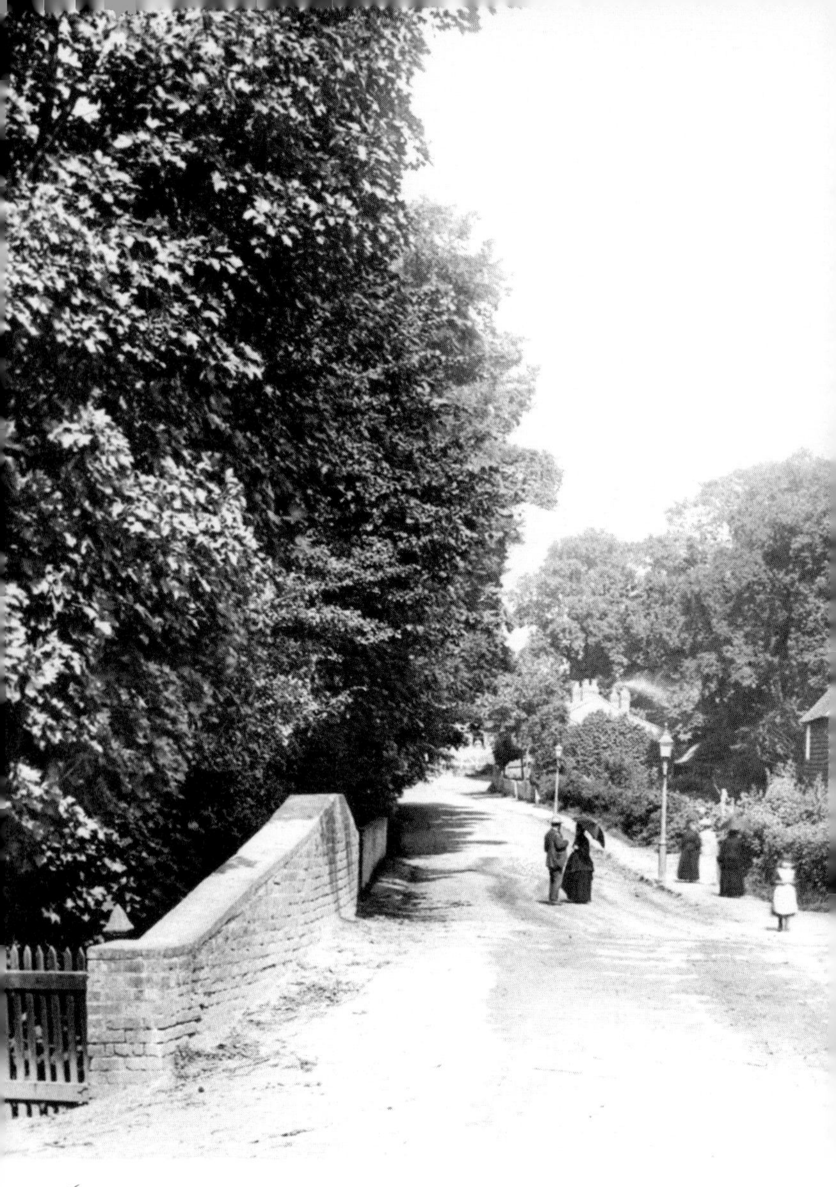

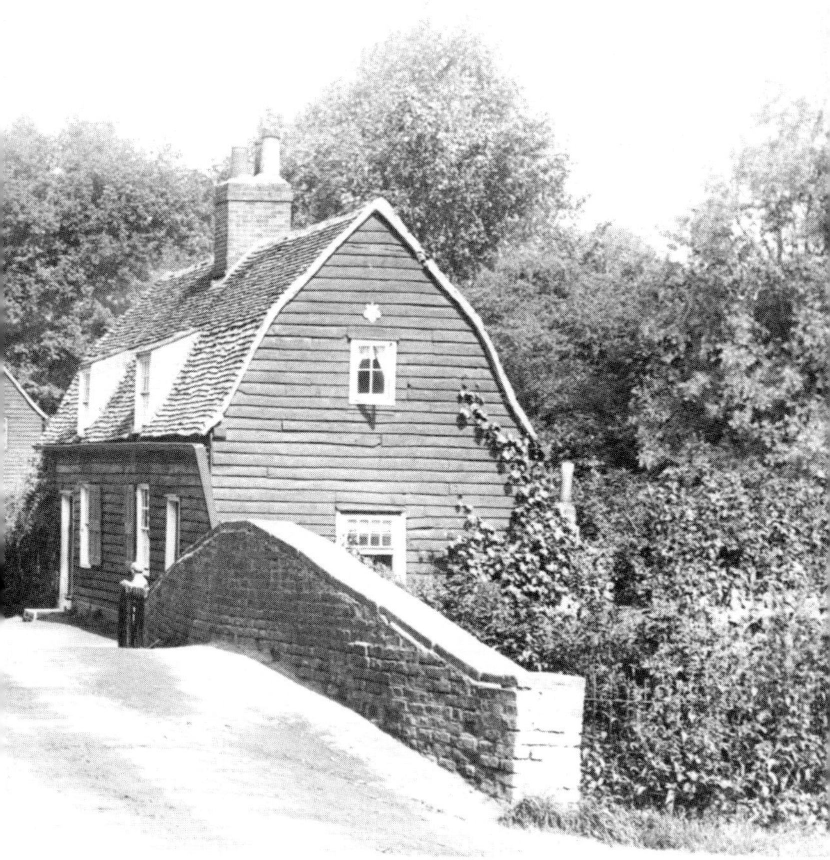

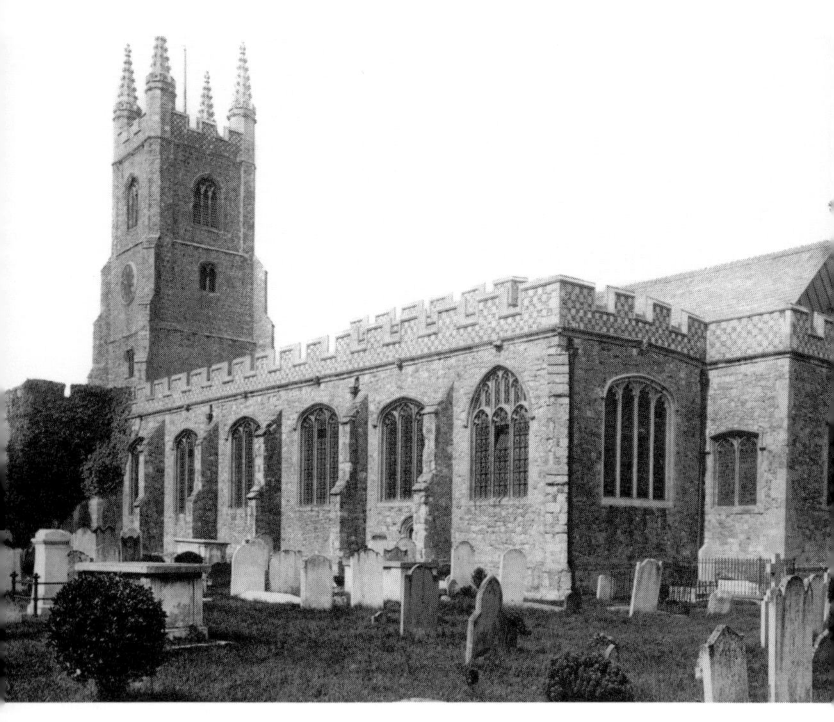

The Church of St Mary stands at the top of the hill above the old Cluniac Priory of Prittlewell. It dates from Norman times, but parts of an older arch, containing some Roman bricks, may be seen in the nave. The large west tower was built in the late 15th century.

PRITTLEWELL
THE CHURCH   1891 / 29075

SOUTHEND

THE OLD PRIORY AND PARK   C1950 / S155023

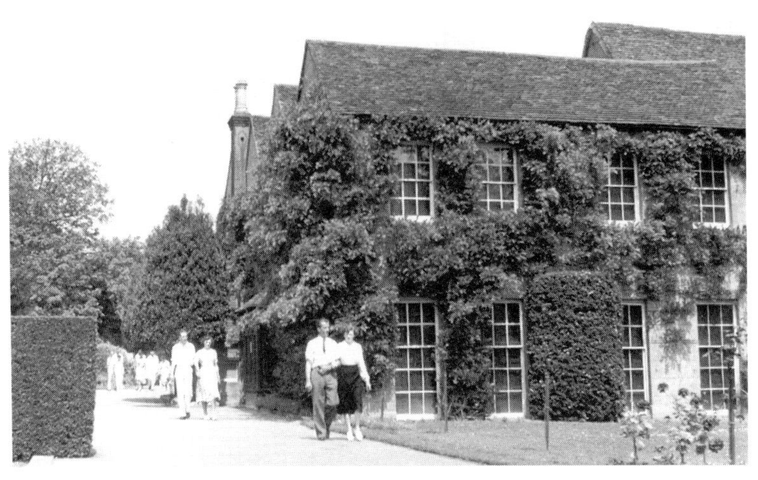

Prittlewell Priory was a victim of the dissolution of the monasteries in 1536. Much of the building has been demolished but the refectory, seen here, remains, as does the Prior's Chamber and the cellar. At the end of the First World War Mr R A Jones purchased the house and grounds. He presented the estate to the town and it was opened to the public by the Duke of York, later King George VI, in 1920.

SOUTHEND

THE PRIORY   C1960 / S155145

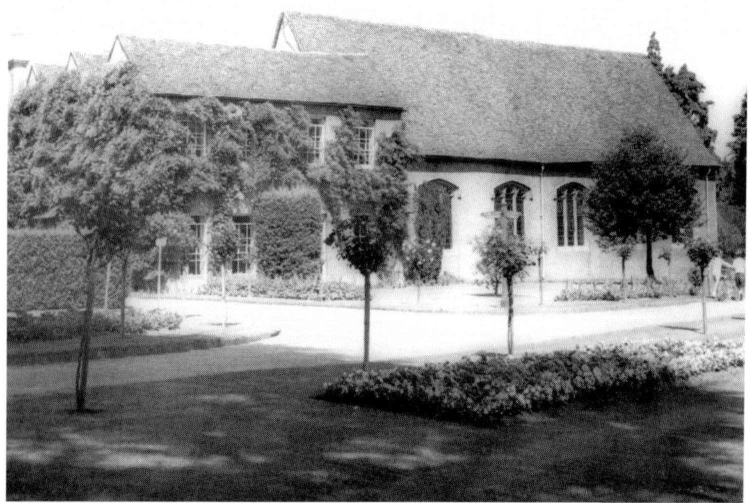

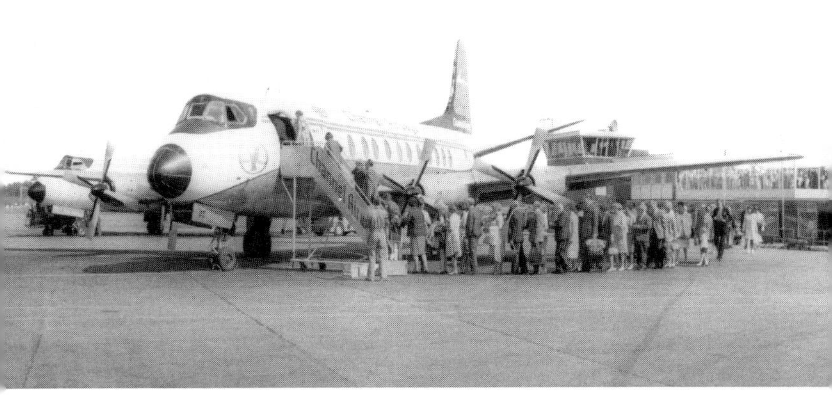

Continuing north, away from the sea, we reach Southend Airport. This was used during both World Wars. By the early 1960s journeys to the Continent were becoming increasingly popular. Here we see a long queue waiting to board this Channel Airways flight, whilst many onlookers watch from the departure building.

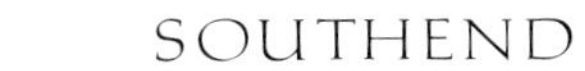

SOUTHEND

THE AIRPORT   c1960 / S155154

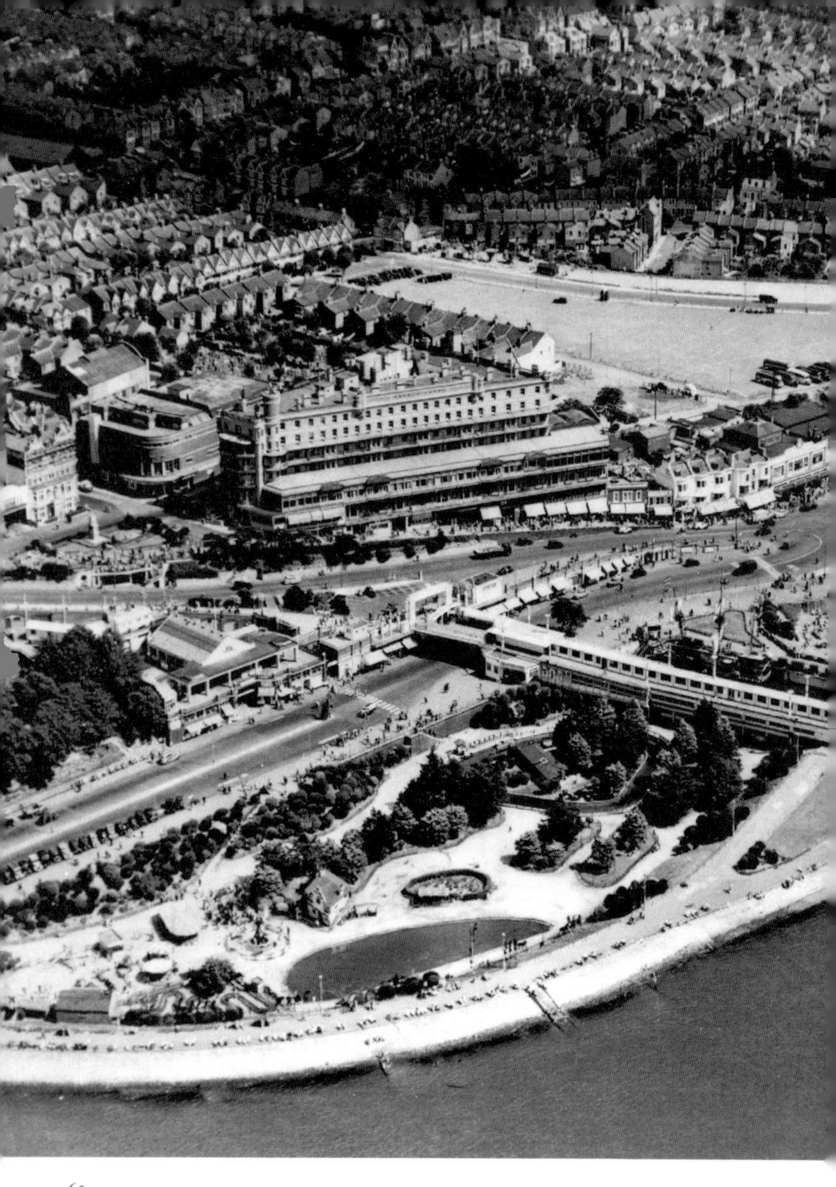

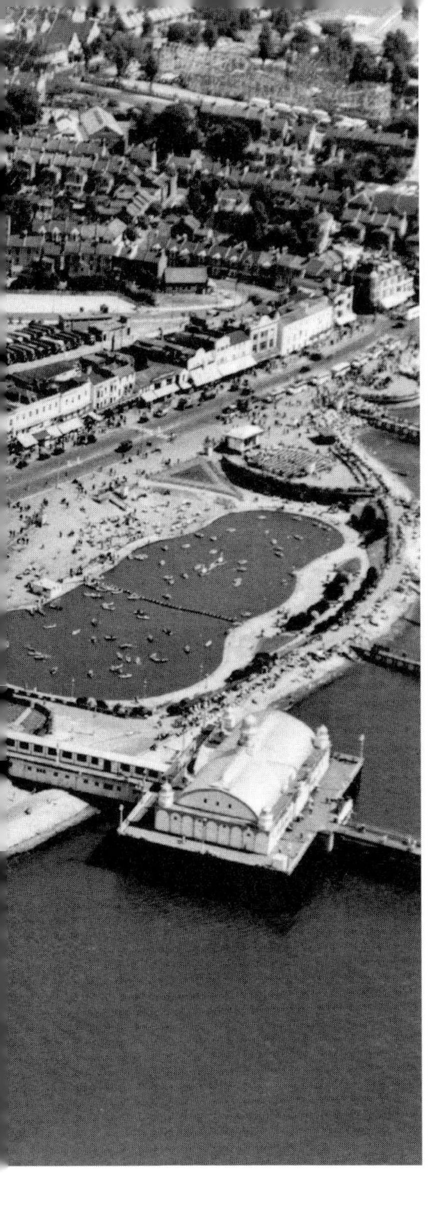

Returning to the seaside once more this view gives an excellent idea of the way in which the town had developed by the middle years of the 20th century. The pier, with its pavilion, is clearly shown with the Palace Hotel rising above Pier Hill. The Ritz Cinema stands behind the hotel. Beyond the large open space can be seen some of the well-ordered housing development behind the sea front, typical of a town that was planned, rather than developed over many centuries. The Boating Lake and Playground dominate the foreground.

SOUTHEND

AN AERIAL VIEW

C1955 / S155044

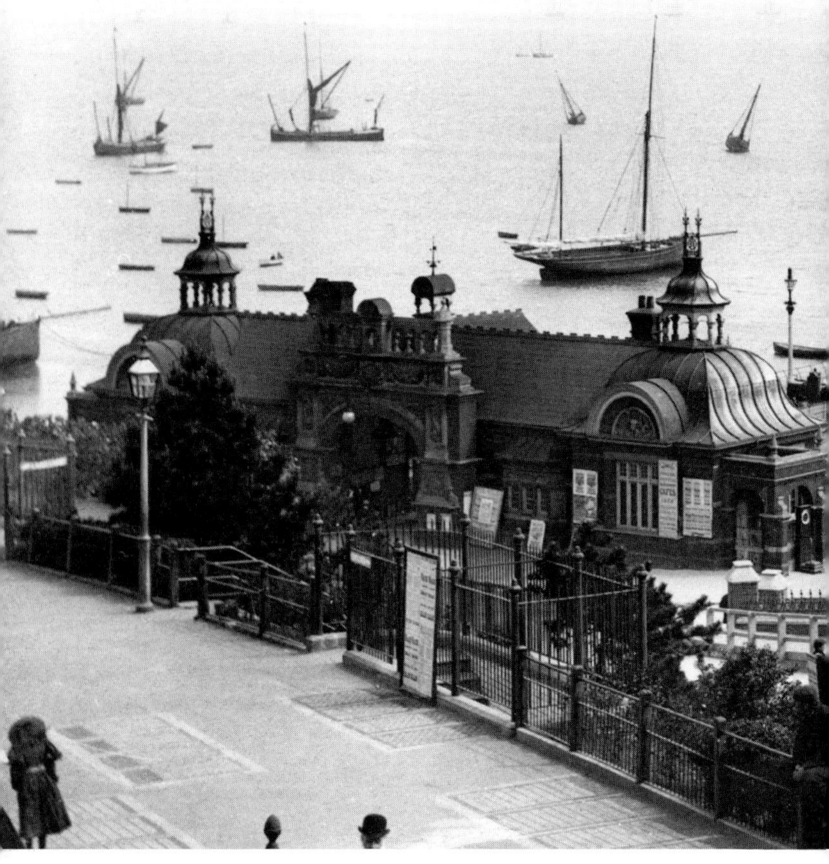

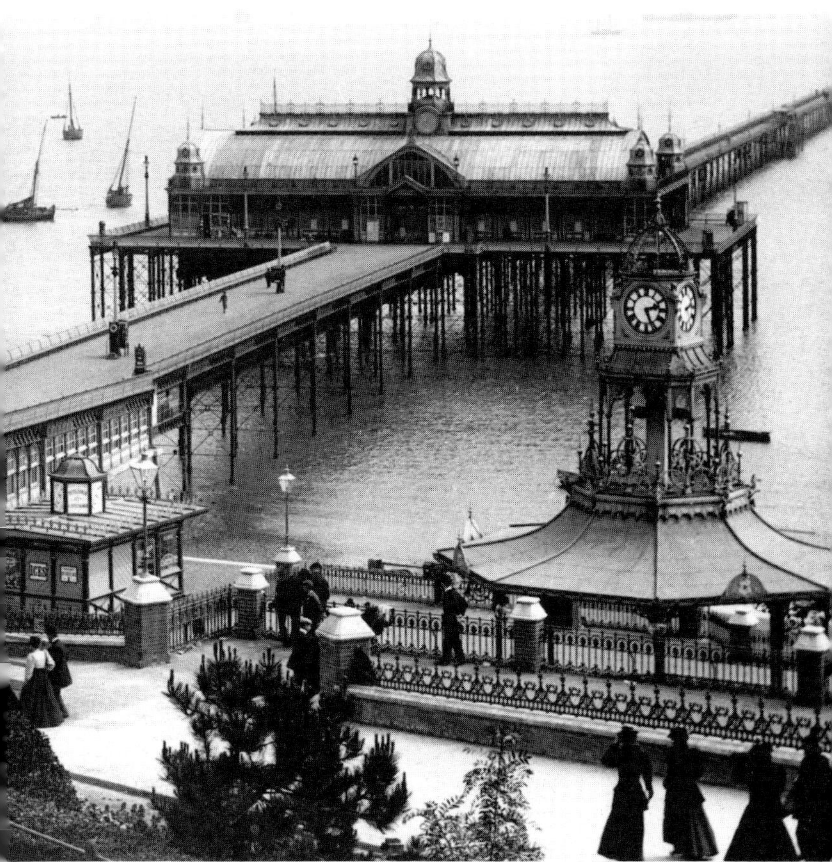

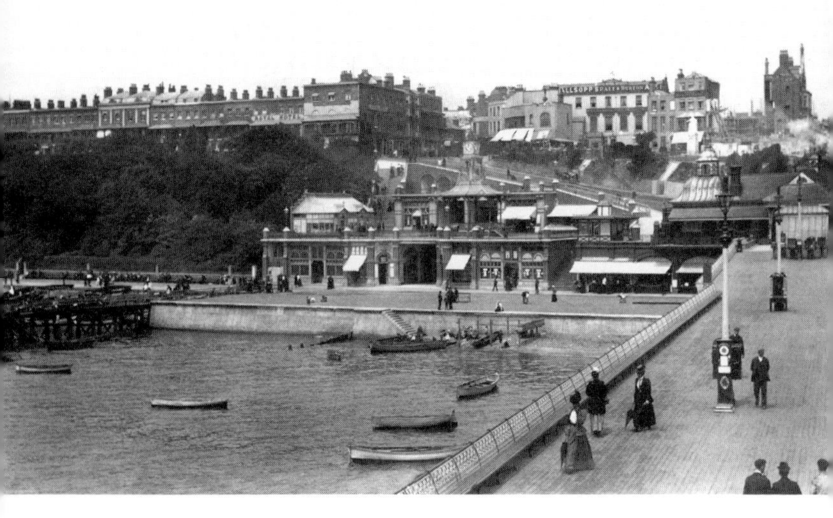

Slot machines can be seen in this picture and there is yet another weighing machine, this time on the pier itself. Wooden buttresses support the Pier Restaurant, on the hill behind Queen Victoria's statue. No one was meant to miss the advertisement for Allsop's Pale and Burton Ales above the hotel. Pier Hill rises towards The Royal Hotel and Royal Terrace.

SOUTHEND

FROM THE PIER   1898 / 41378

In the background of this picture stands the Gas Works jetty. Pier Hill leads down to the sea front esplanade, with the Palace Hotel on the left. Below the hotel, facing the sea, are many small shops. Towards the bottom of the hill The Gaiety Bazaar may be seen, a treasure-house for holiday gifts. Nearby the well-known Rossi ice creams are sold. A notice close to the zebra crossing advertises a Bingo Palace.

SOUTHEND
PIER HILL   c1960 / S155086

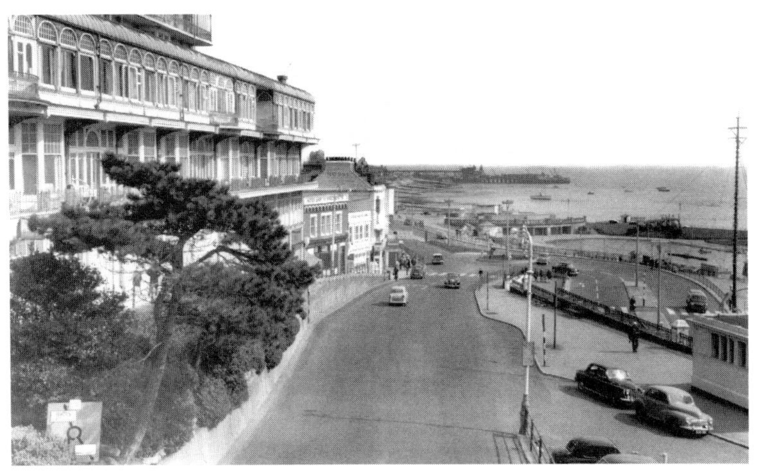

The Pier Pavilion, once popular for concert parties and ballroom dancing, is now being used for roller skating.   The Big Wheel can be seen in the playground to the right of the picture, with The Golden Hind to the left.

SOUTHEND

THE PIER   C1955 / S155068

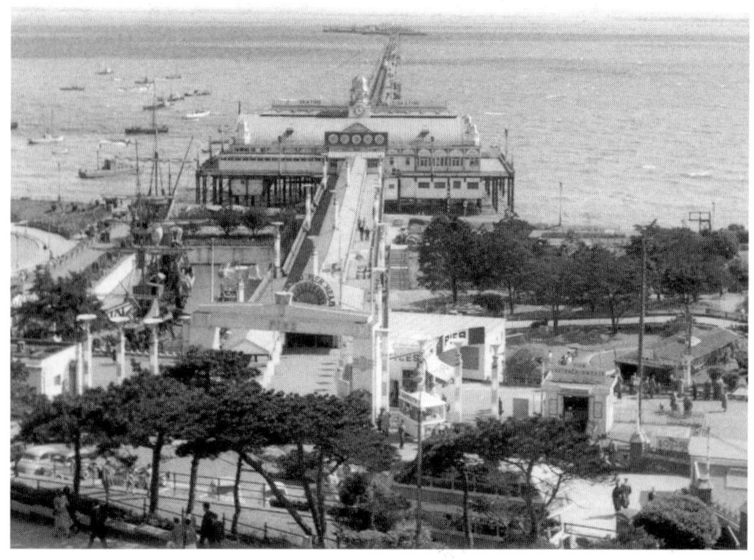

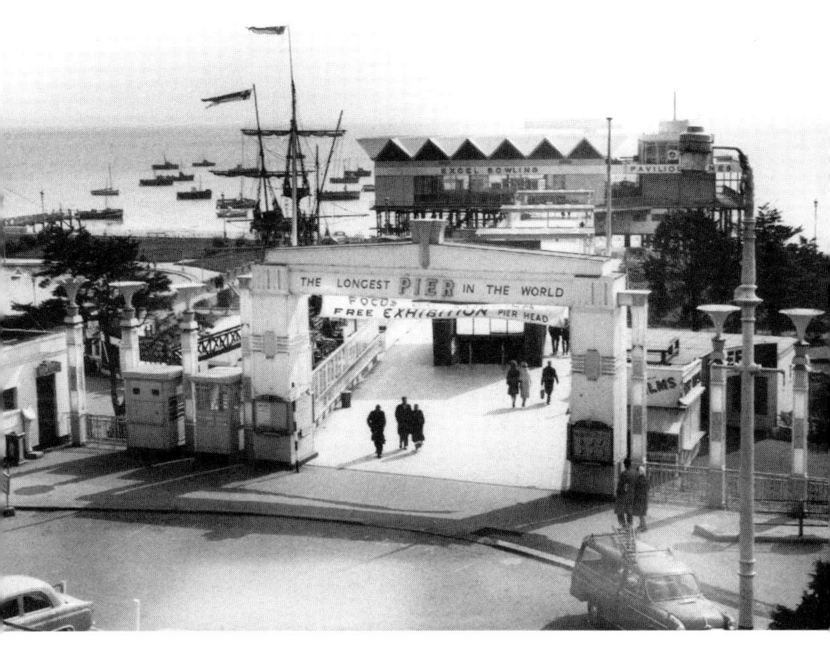

'Focus On America' is advertised as a free exhibition at the pier head. Such exhibitions always pulled in large crowds. Ten Pin Bowling has become a popular pastime and brought many enthusiasts to the Excel Pavilion Bowling Lanes.

SOUTHEND

THE PIER   C1962 / S155085

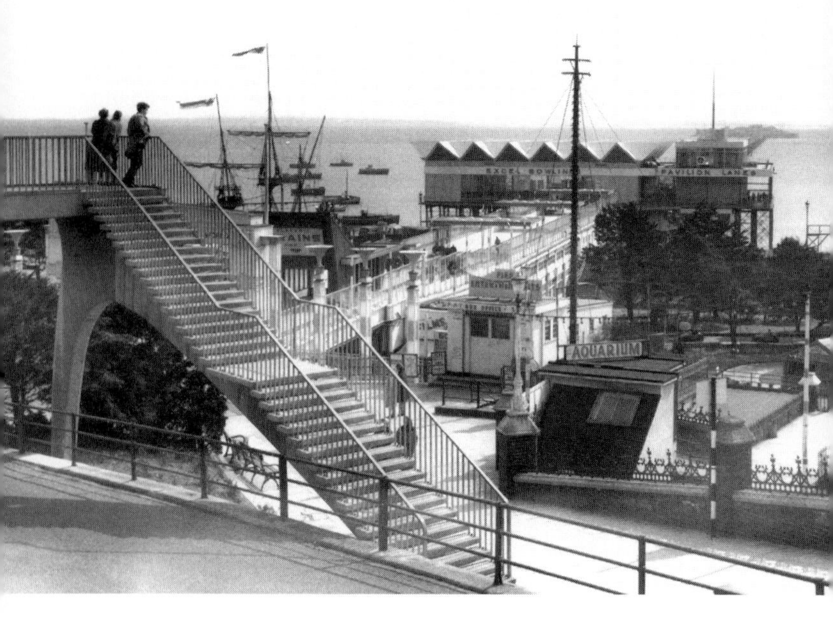

The old Pier Pavilion was burnt down in 1959. The Exel Bowling Lanes replaced it and live entertainment moved to the end of the pier. Steps lead up to a passenger bridge crossing over the busy Pier Hill. The small Aquarium was a popular attraction at this time, with the box office to the left selling tickets for pier entertainments.

SOUTHEND

THE PIER FROM PIER HILL   C1962 / S155084

SOUTHEND

THE BEACH   1898 / 40912

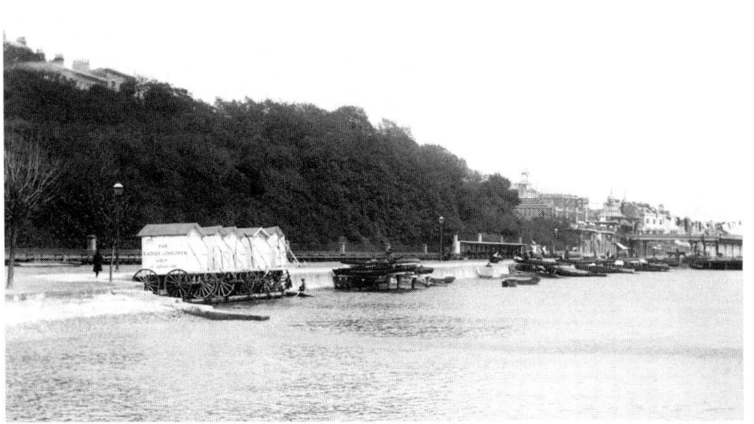

SOUTHEND

FROM THE PIER   C1898 / 41379

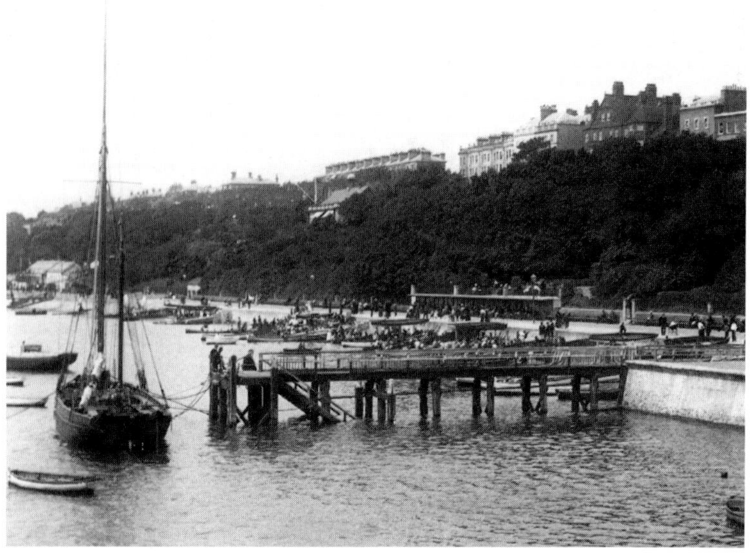

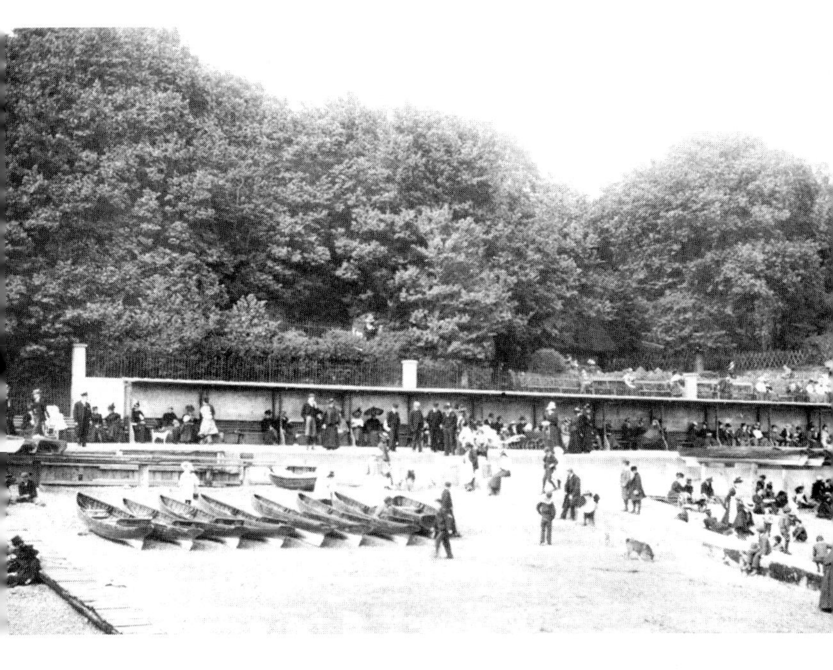

The photographer has moved in closer to the beach to take this picture, although still concentrating on the same area as the former one. The Shrubbery Gardens, above the sun shelter, are well used with plenty of wooden benches. These Victorian children are obviously enjoying their time on the beach. A number of the gentlemen are elegantly dressed with boaters to finish off their seaside apparel.

SOUTHEND

THE BEACH 1898 / 41384

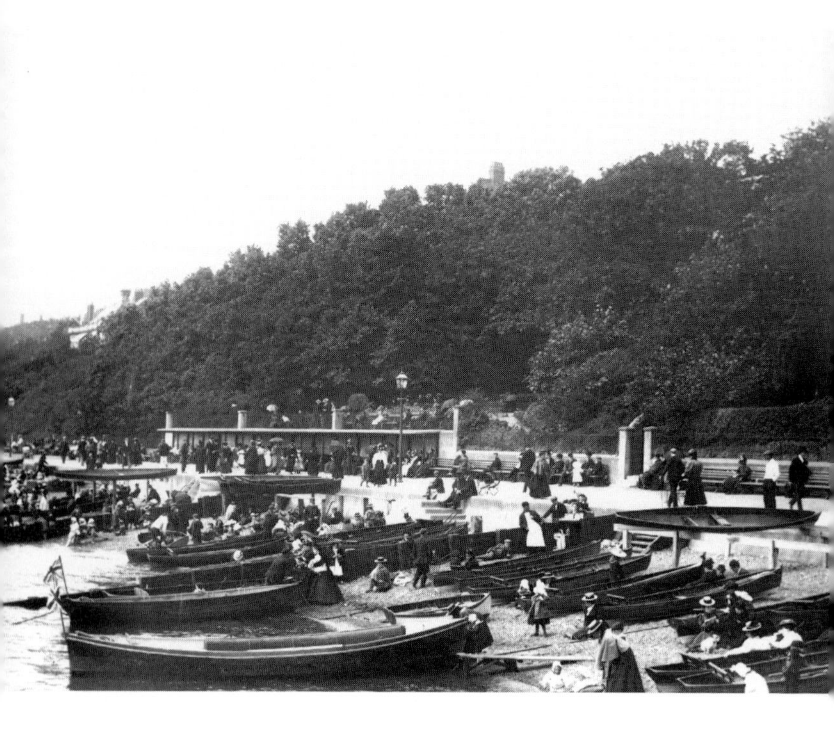

In this busy scene beached boats occupy most of the shingle. However, mothers and children manage to find space and the boats form useful back-rests. The promenade is well used by walkers. Straw hats are popular for both men and women.

SOUTHEND

THE BEACH 1898 / 41383

SOUTHEND

THE BEACH 1898 / 40911

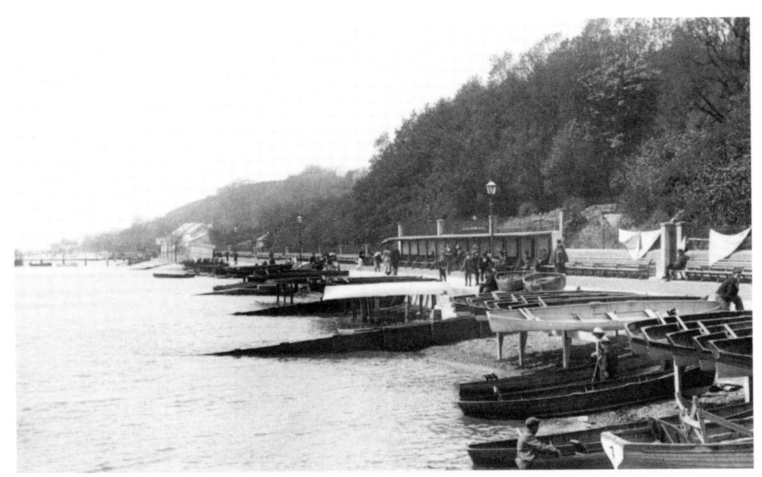

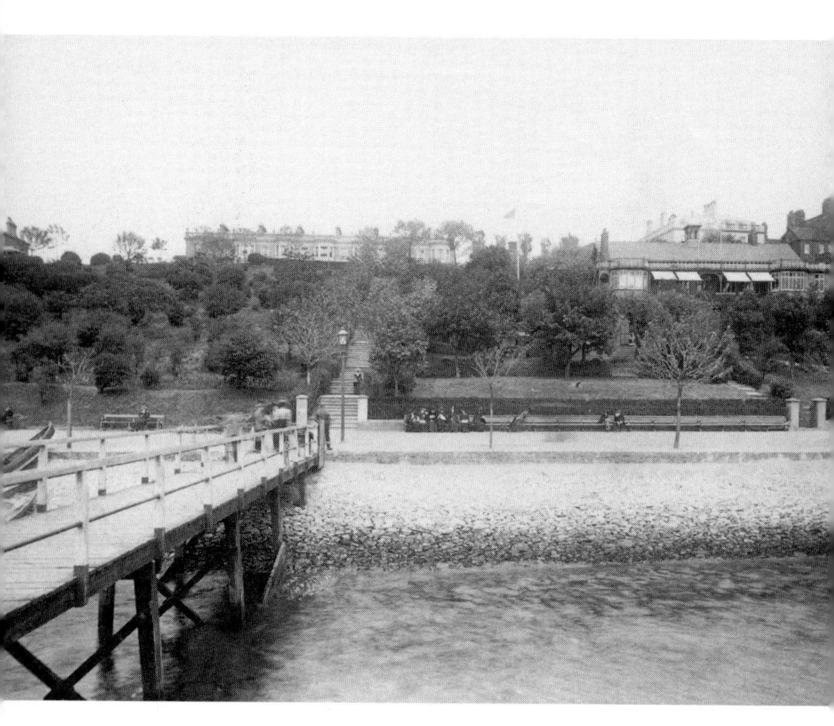

The wooden jetty on the left would have been used at high tide. This photograph was taken long before the widening of the promenade. Most of those enjoying the sea air do so from the comfort of the long line of wooden seats below the cliffs.

SOUTHEND

THE BEACH   1898 / 41381

Here we have a peaceful scene looking towards Westcliff. A mobile jetty is ready for use. This beach is far less crowded than those shown in the 1950s, the Indian Summer of the British seaside town. The couple in the deckchairs sit just above the high tide mark, shown by the line of seaweed.

SOUTHEND

THE BEACH   c1960 / S155133

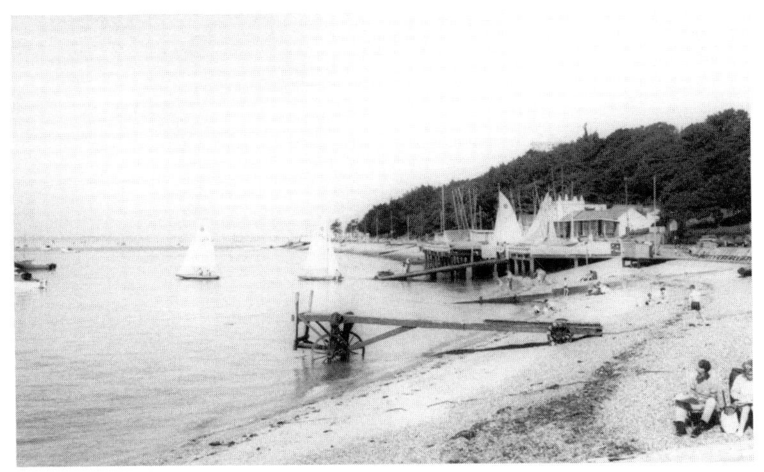

The Shrubbery Gardens, shown in the above picture, were first enclosed in 1825. Here, those staying in Royal Terrace or at The Royal Hotel, could walk in peace, or linger for a while on one of the benches provided. Pier Hill can be seen rising behind the foreshore buildings with the High Street stretching north from The Royal Hotel.

SOUTHEND

FROM THE PIER   1898 / 41380

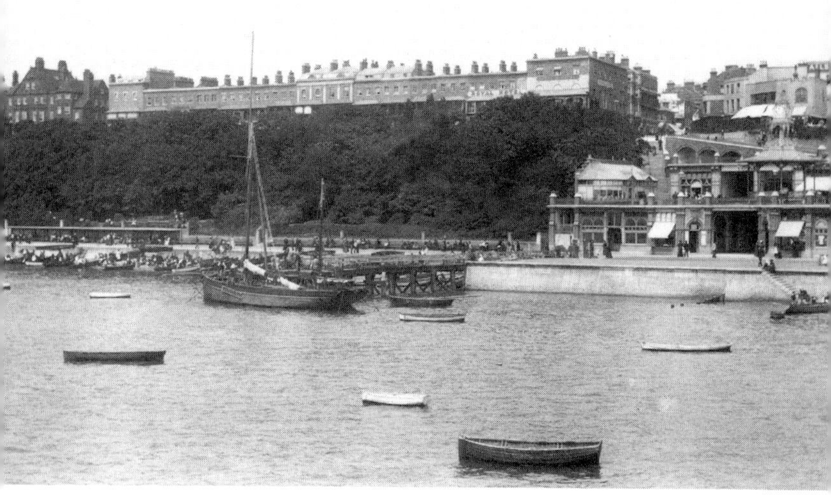

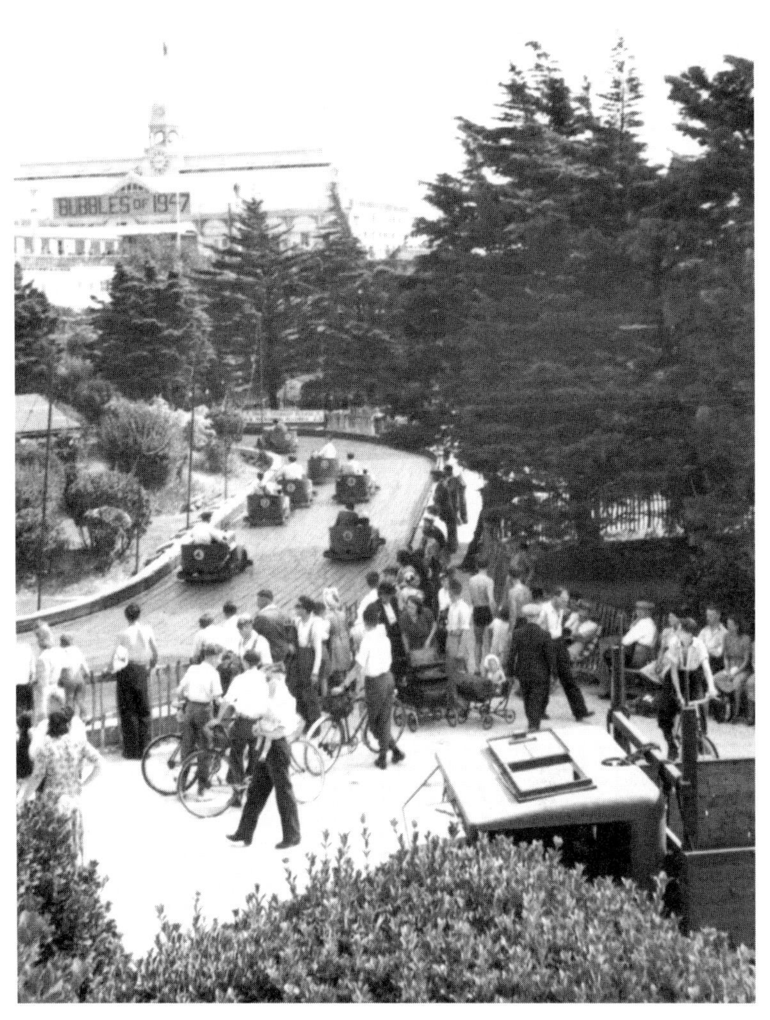

SOUTHEND

THE MINIATURE RACE TRACK   1947 / S155012

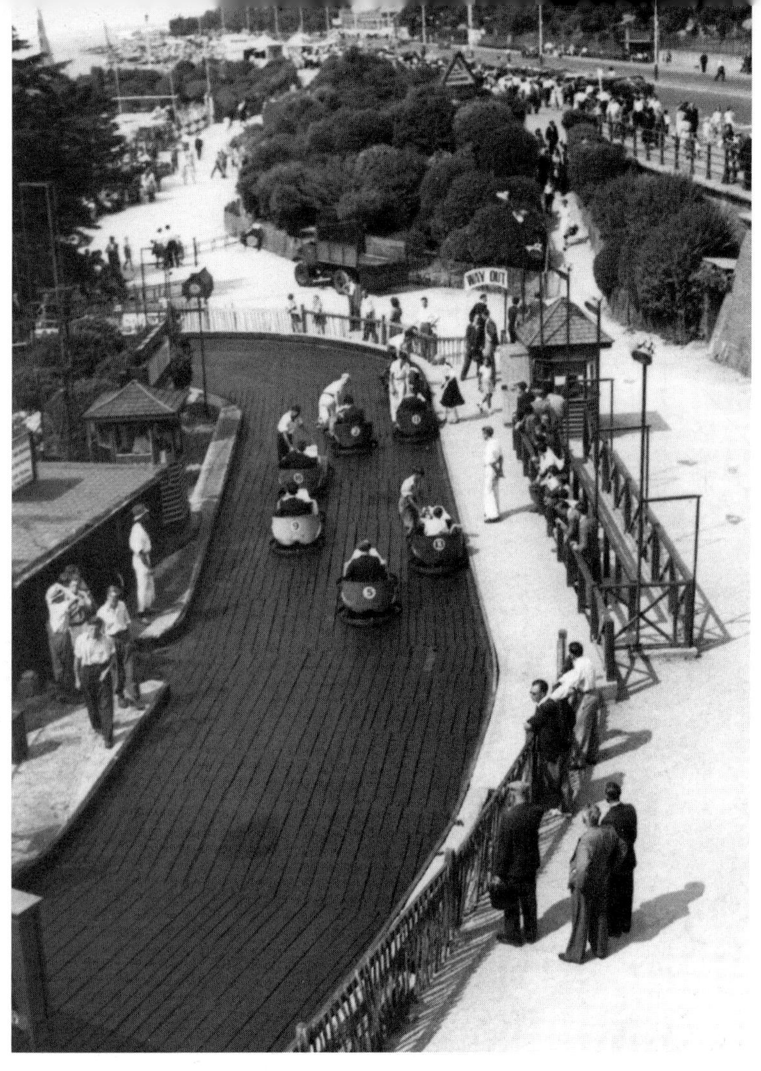

SOUTHEND

THE PROMENADE AND AMUSEMENT PARK   1947 / S155010

With the tide in swimmers can enjoy the water. The breakwaters were much loved by children as shingle built up on one side, leaving the other much lower. Unsuspecting visitors could be caught out, if not warned in advance about this drop. Sloping concrete blocks act as sea protection.

SOUTHEND

THE BEACH FROM THE PIER   1947 / S155011

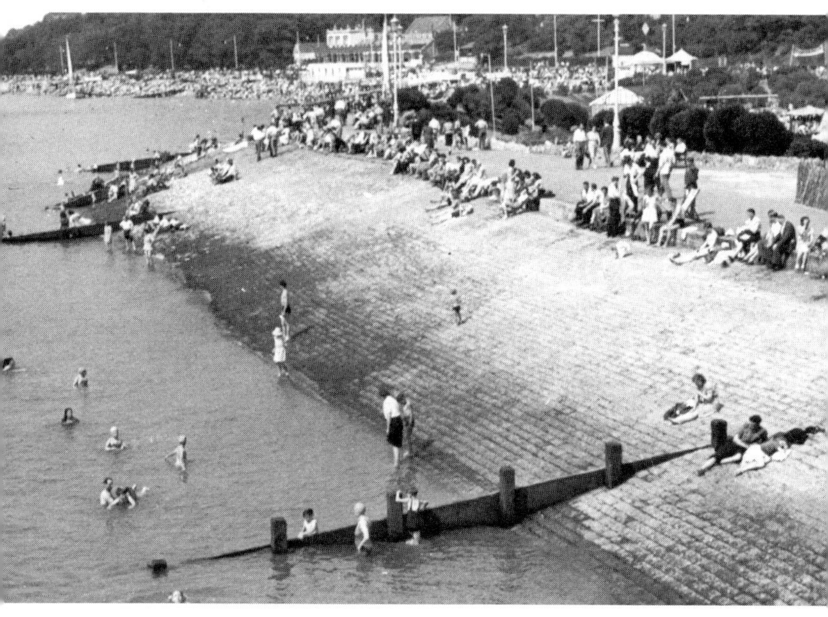

Royal Terrace with the Royal Hotel on the eastern corner can clearly be seen at the top of the cliffs. Boats are drawn up on the beach close to the promenade. The foreshore buildings near to the pier include a small bandstand, suitable for open air concerts.

SOUTHEND

FROM THE PIER   1898 / 40910

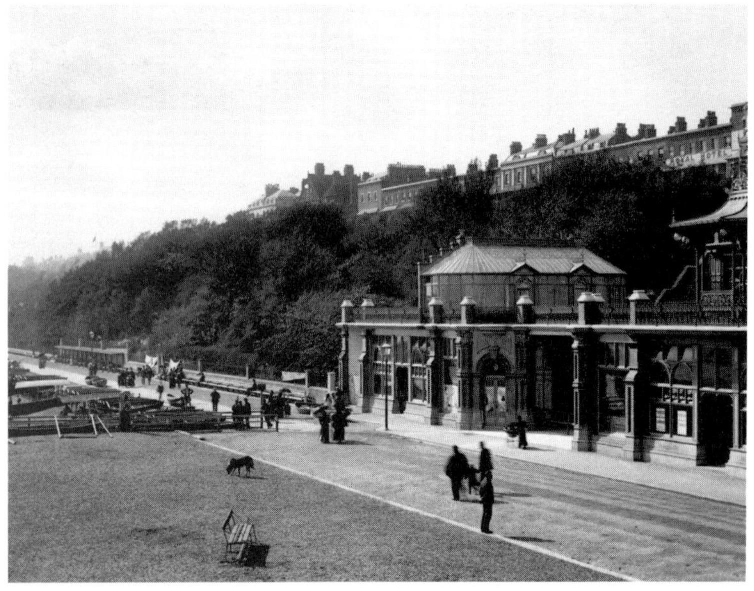

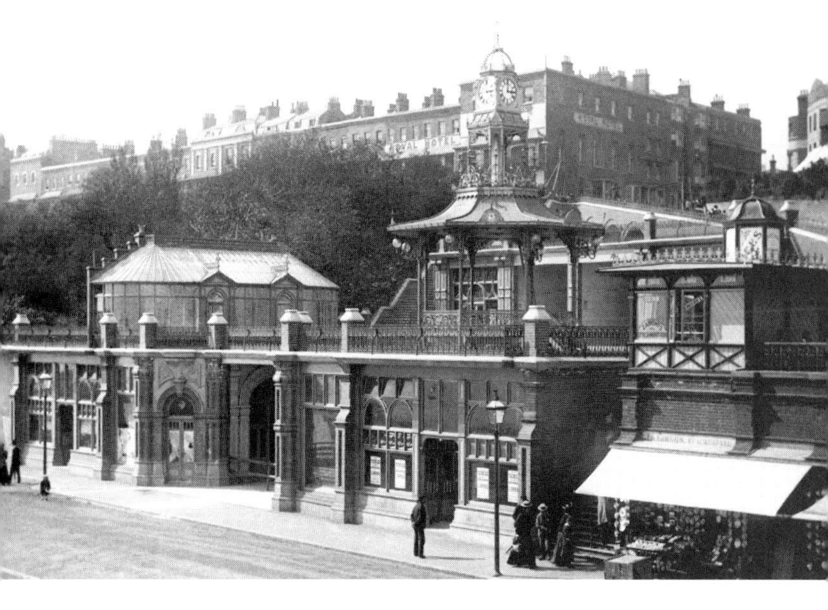

Pier Hill rises behind these foreshore buildings. The clock tower surmounts the concert hall cum bandstand. This was demolished in the early 1930s. Ices, always popular at the seaside, are advertised above Zanchi's Refreshment Room on the right. Below is L Goings Beach Bazaar, with some of its wares displayed on the pavement.

SOUTHEND

PIER HILL BUILDINGS   1898 / 40909

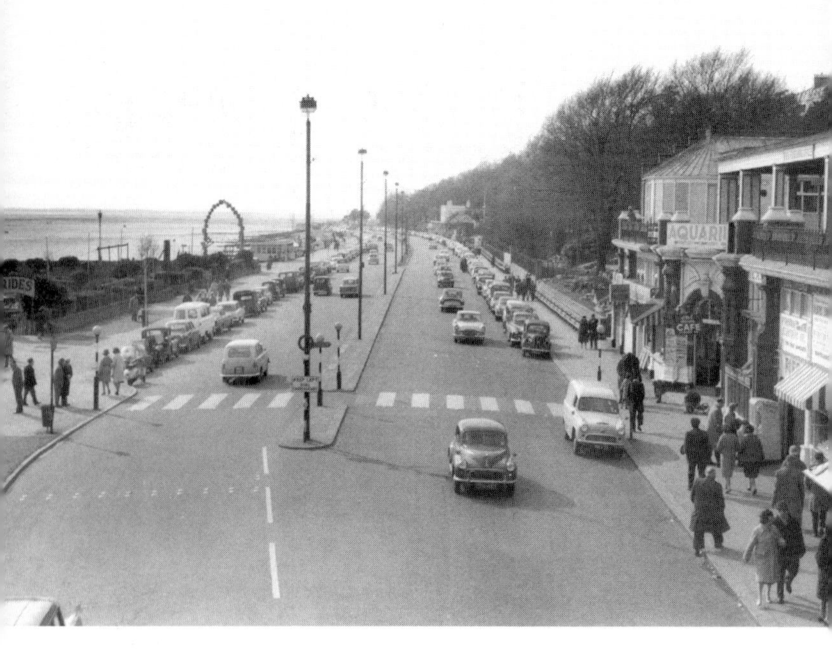

This photograph was taken in the same area as 40909. Now, a wide road and Peter Pan's Playground cover what was once the beach. Many of the buildings on the right have changed little in outward appearance, although most have become busy shops protected by awnings. By 1960 more visitors were arriving by car, as can be seen from the well-parked kerb. Beyond the Aquarium are the trees of the Shrubbery Gardens.

SOUTHEND

THE PROMENADE   c1960 / S155081

*Many of the old buildings seen at the entrance
to the pier in earlier pictures had disappeared
by this time. Steamer cruises had been popular
for some years, with the Eagle Line taking
passengers on day trips from the pier head.
Pier Hill is busy with pedestrians but they
seem untroubled by cars.*

SOUTHEND

THE PIER   1947 / S155009

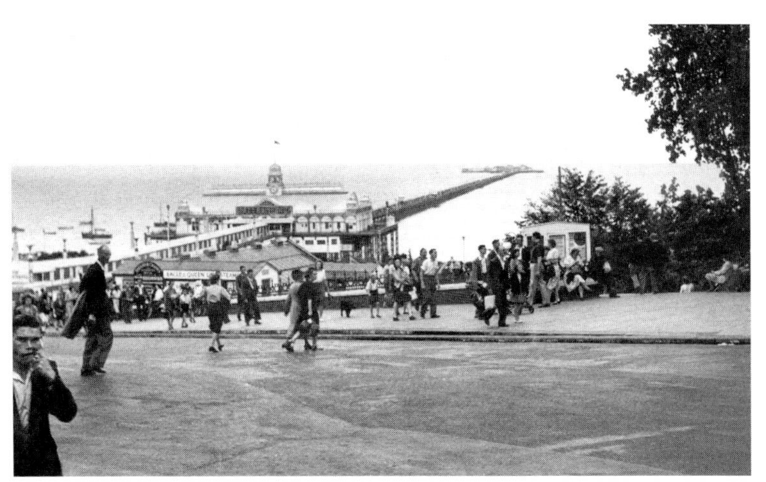

The lights have been hung ready for the summer illuminations. The pier was always a spectacular sight at this time of year. Well-wrapped holidaymakers manage to enjoy the sun on the ever-popular deckchairs. Ten-Pin Bowling is played in the new pavilion. Pleated skirts, of the type worn by the two young ladies at the front of the picture, were fashionable at this time.

SOUTHEND

THE PIER   C1962 / S155102

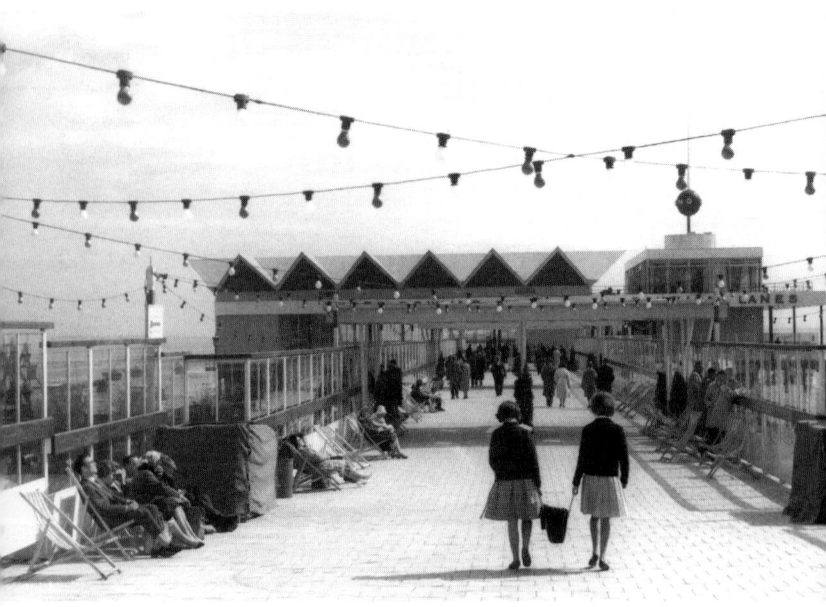

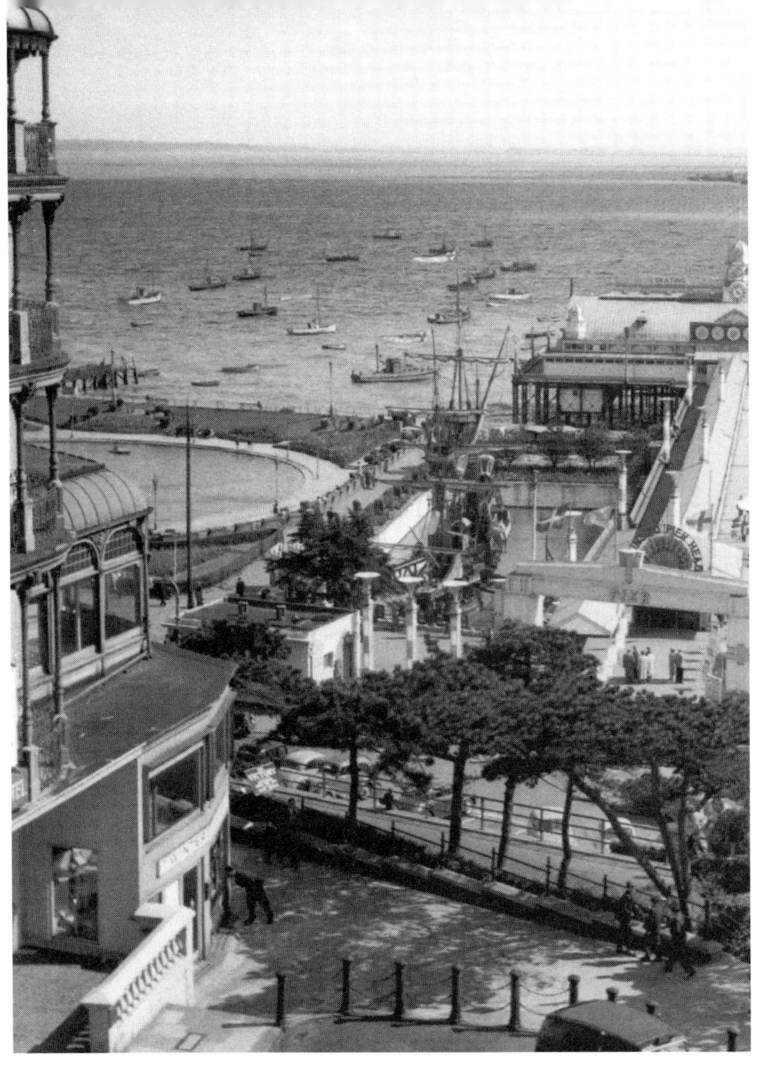

SOUTHEND

THE PIER   C1955 / S155071

SOUTHEND

THE GOLDEN HIND AND PIER   C1950 / S155033

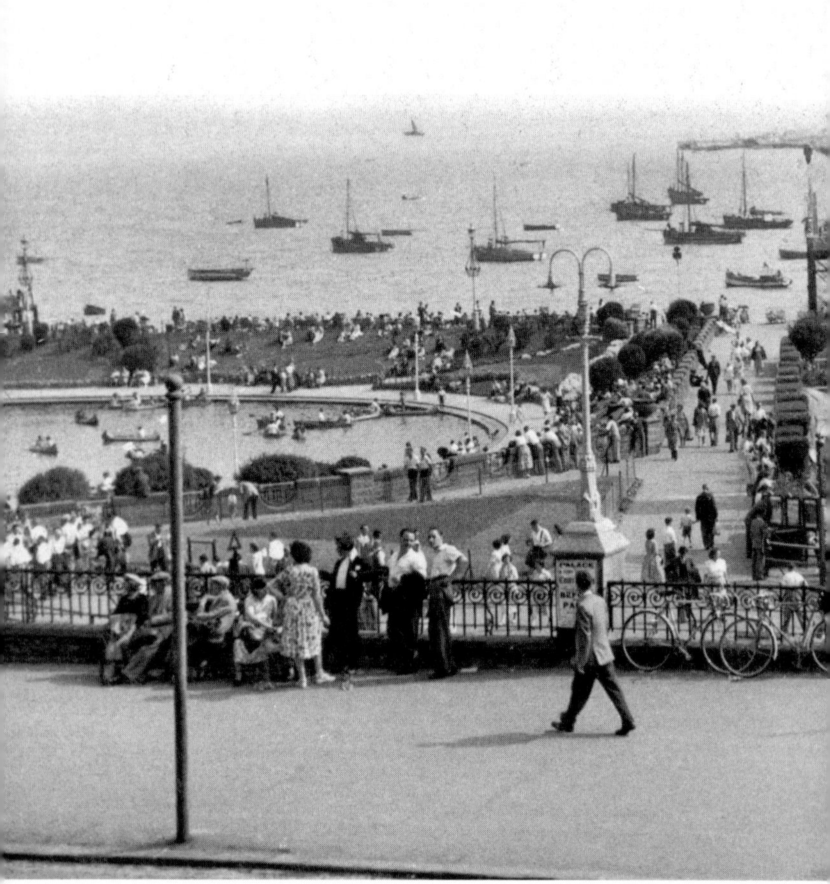

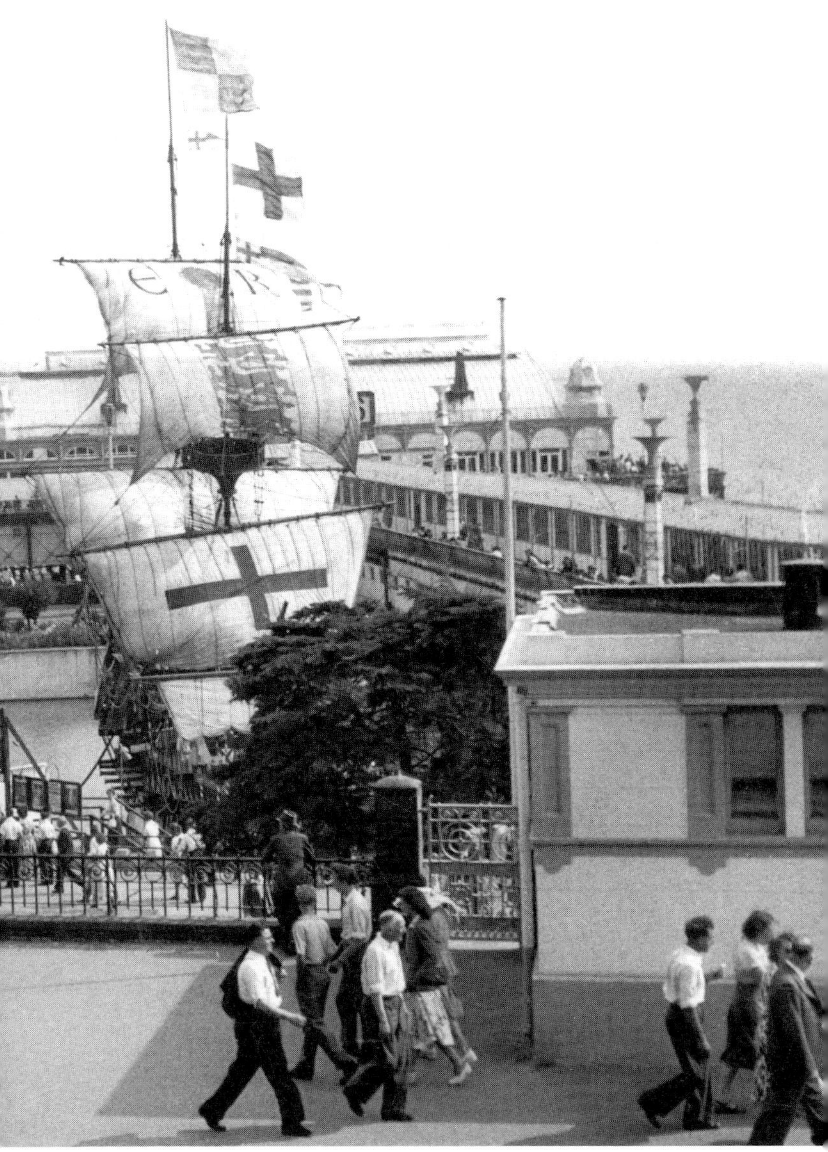

Visitors crowd the pavement and queue to board this popular and impressive attraction. The summer entertainment, 'Bubbles', is advertised on the Pier Pavilion. Those walking on the pier have a good view of the activities below.

SOUTHEND

THE GALLEON   C1950 / S155035

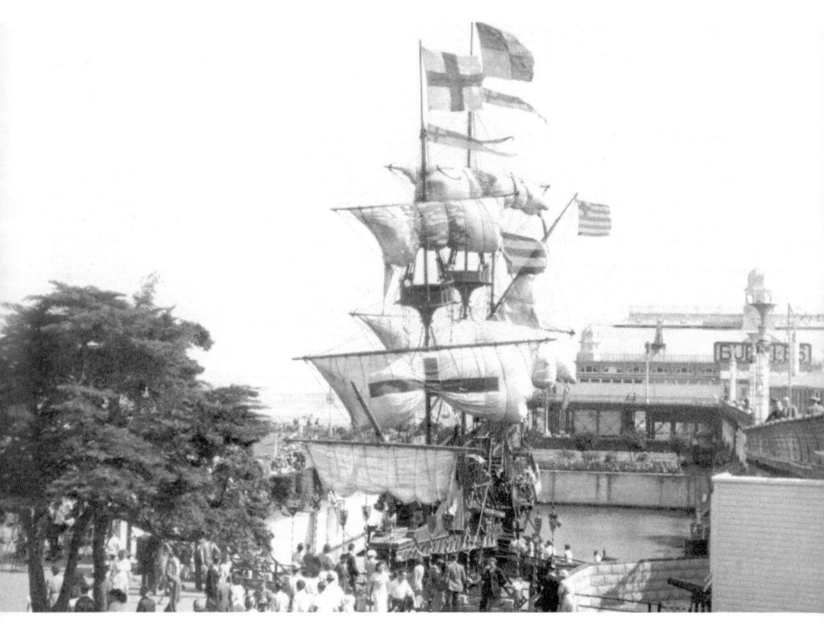

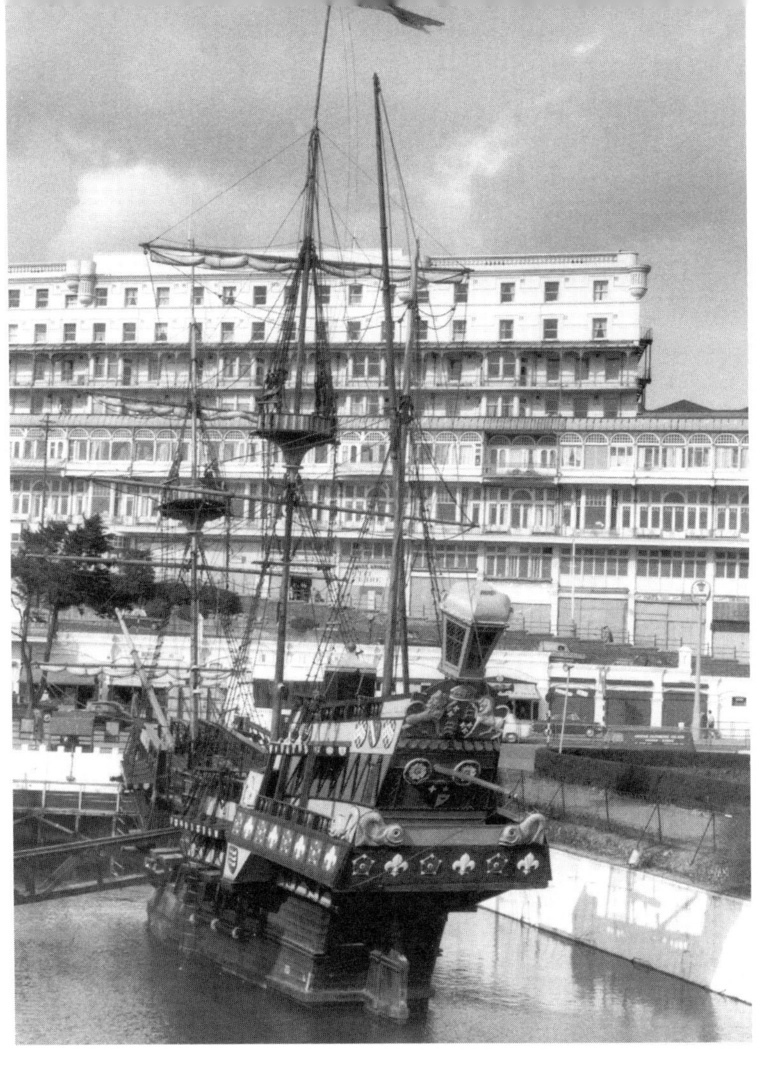

SOUTHEND
THE GOLDEN HIND c1960 / S155079

SOUTHEND

THE GOLDEN HIND   C1950 / S155038

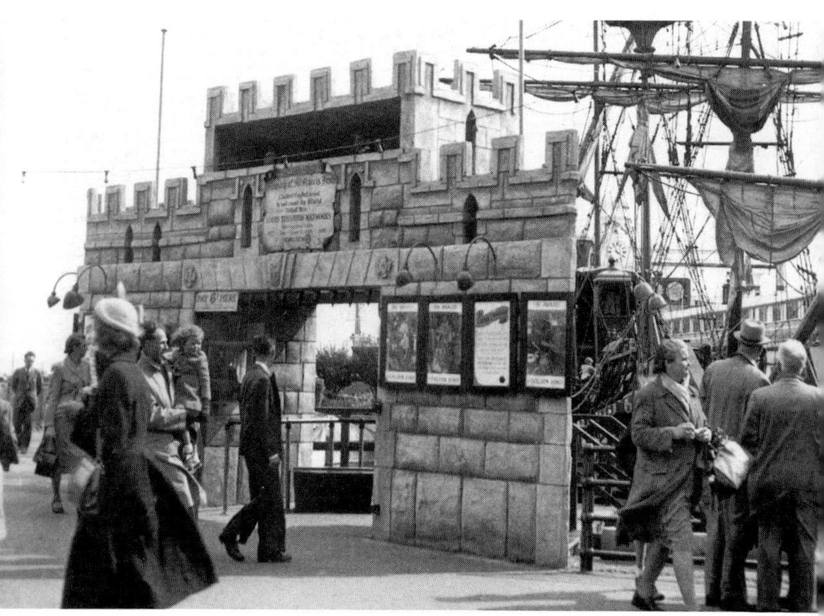

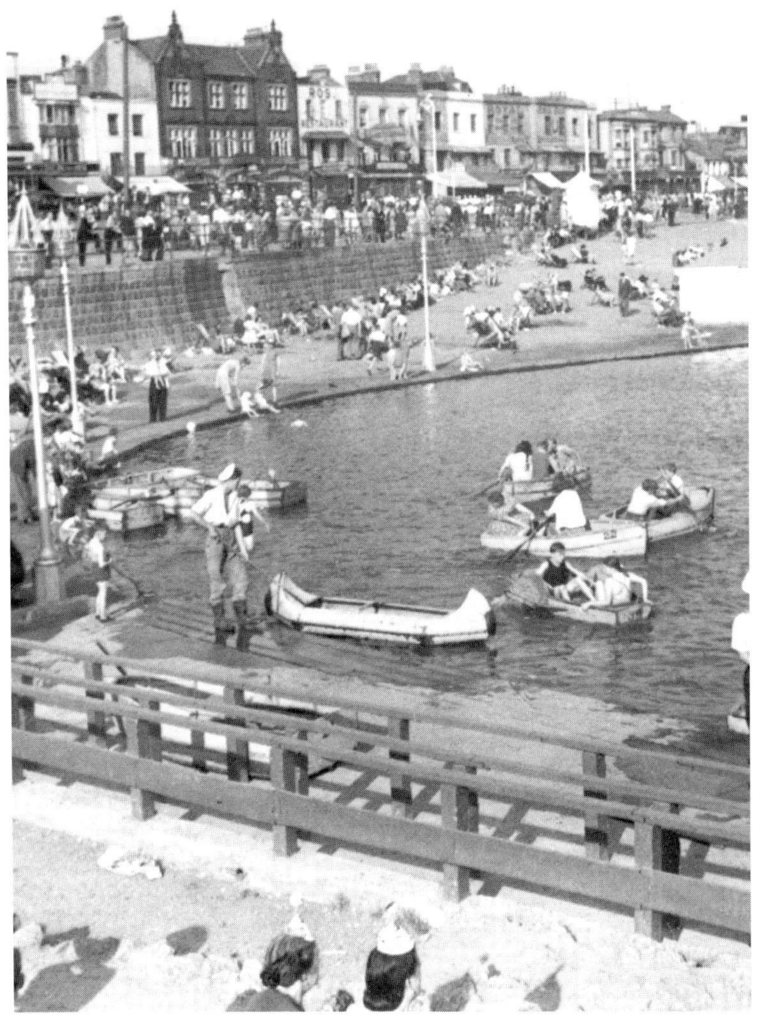

SOUTHEND

THE BOATING LAKE   c1945 / S155006

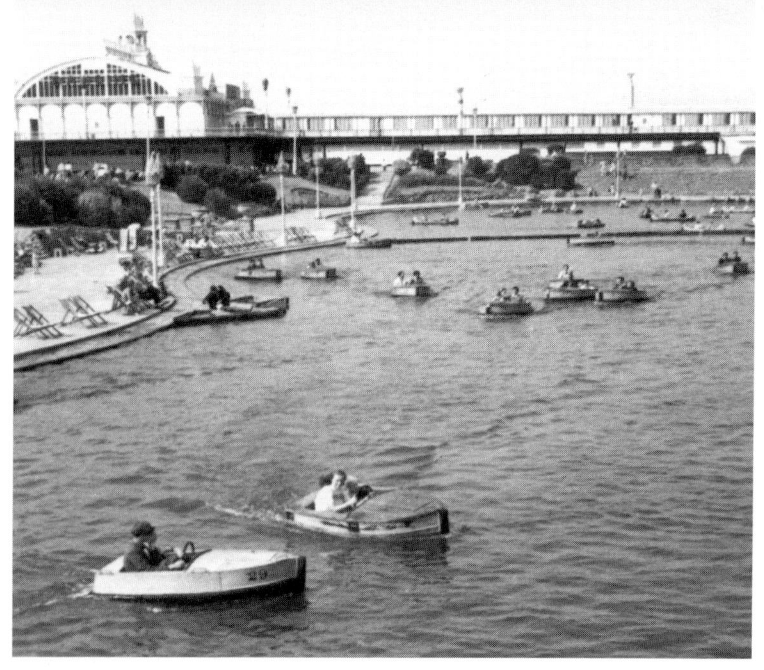

This pool was to the east of the pier. Motor boats can be seen in the foreground but the pool was split in two. Canoes and rowing boats could be hired on the part closer to the pier. The Victorian Pier Pavilion can be seen in the background.

SOUTHEND

THE CHILDREN'S POOL   C1945 / S155003

This view of the busy sea front, looking west across the boating lake, shows Pier Hill rising up towards the Royal Hotel and Royal Parade. The Olympia advertises 'Two Great Bands, Twice Daily'. Next door are the rounded bays over shops and beyond the imposing bulk of the Palace Hotel.

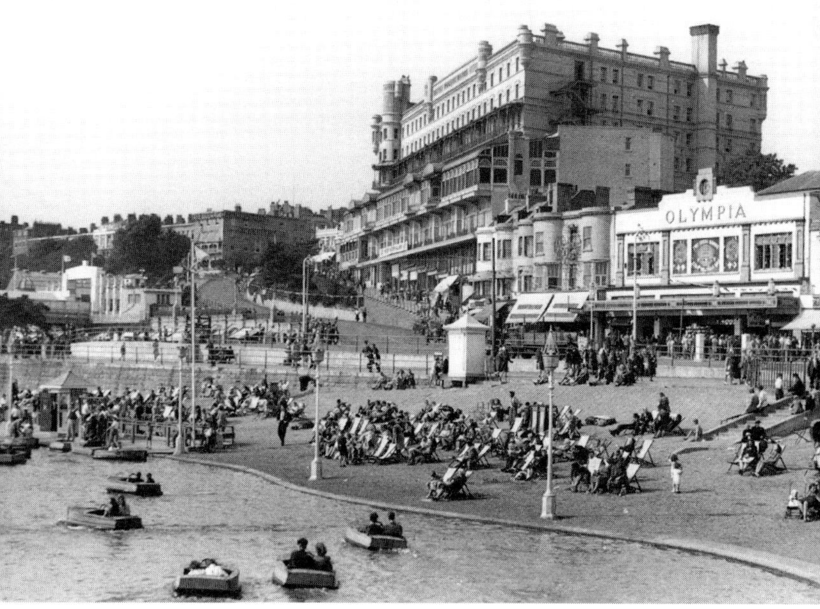

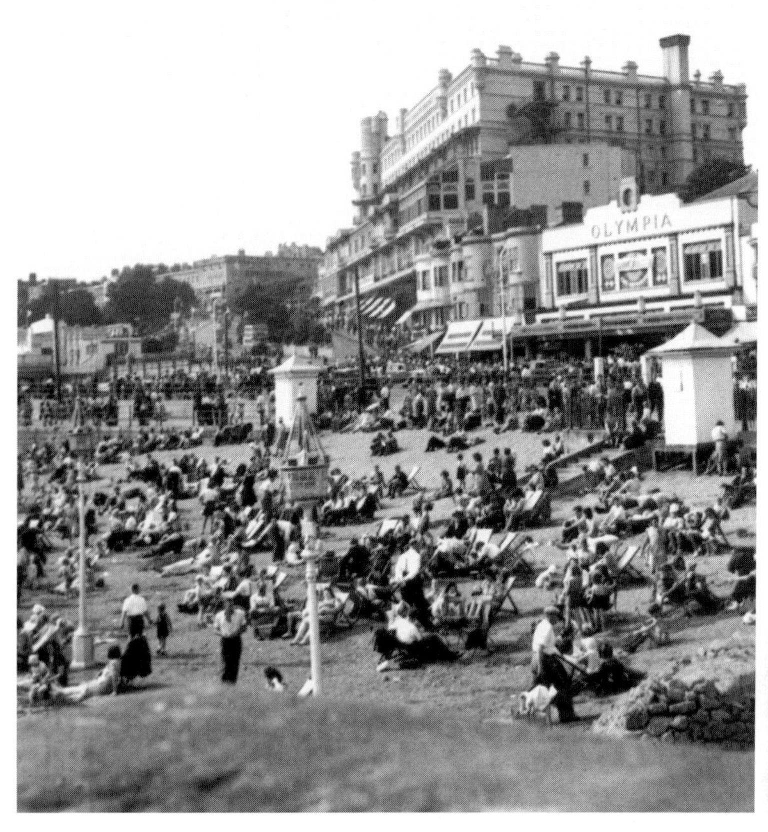

SOUTHEND

THE PALACE HOTEL AND BEACH   c1950 / S155013

SOUTHEND

MARINE PARADE   1898 / 41382

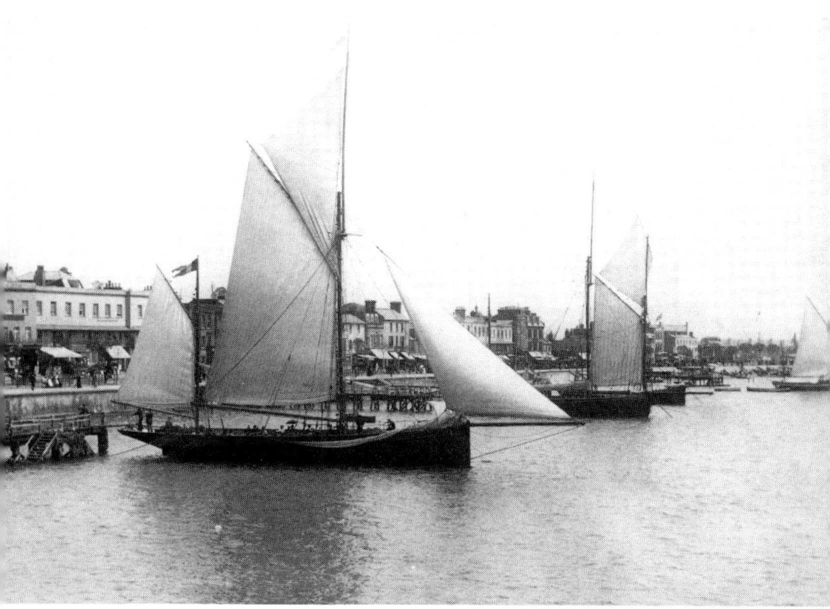

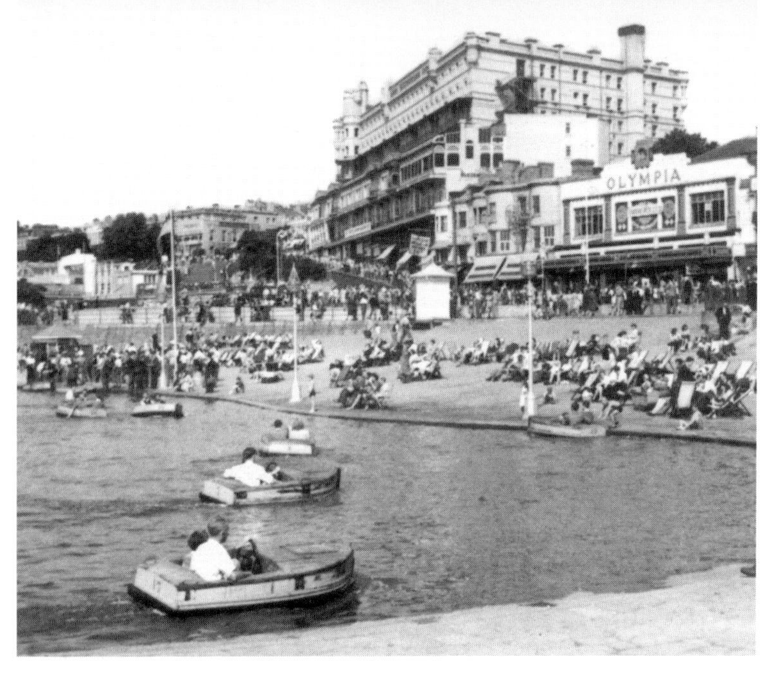

The huge Palace Hotel was built in 1904. At first named The Metropole, it served as Queen Mary's Naval Hospital during the First World War. Then, for many years, it served as a popular hotel. In recent years its role has changed, being used at one time for apartments for senior citizens and more recently to house the homeless. The boating lake was a well-used amusement in the 1950s.

SOUTHEND

THE PALACE HOTEL AND BEACH   C1950 / S155001

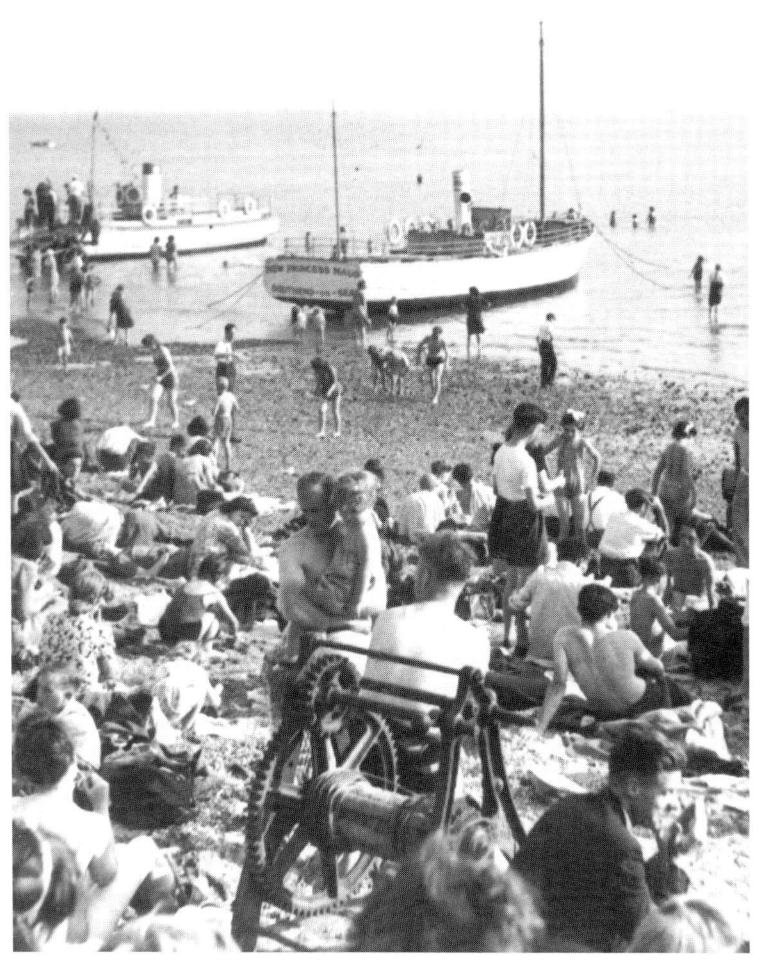

SOUTHEND

THE BEACH   c1945 / S155004

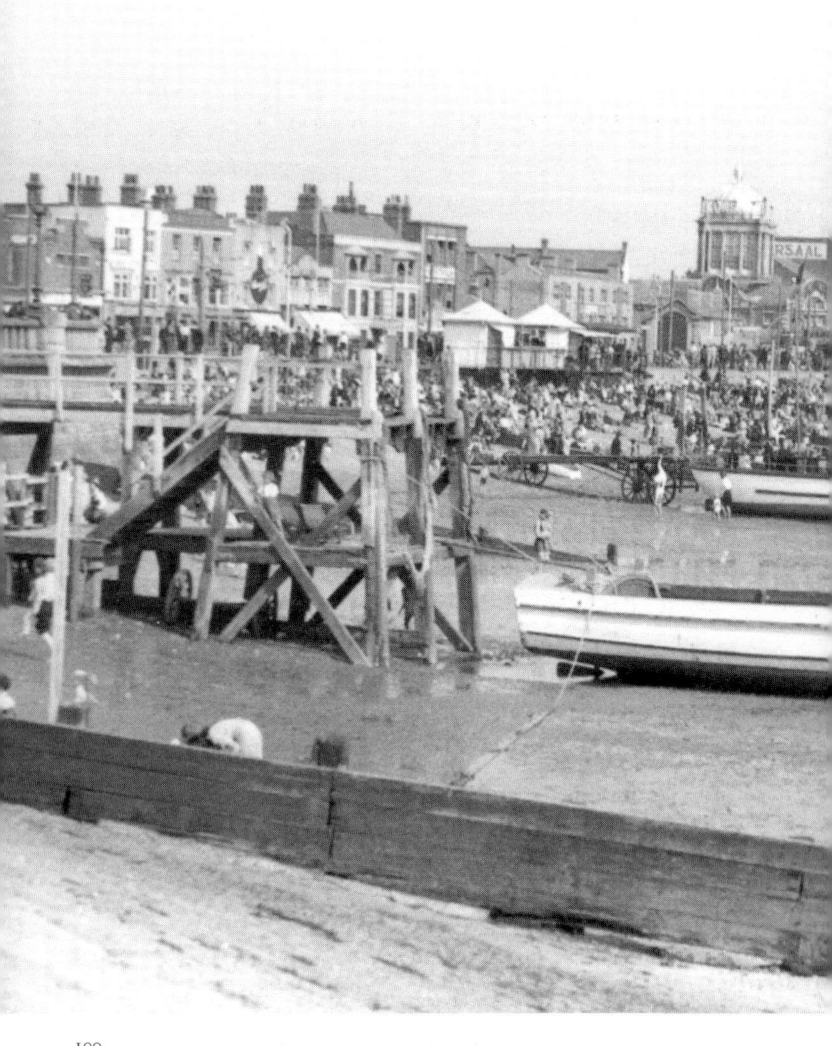

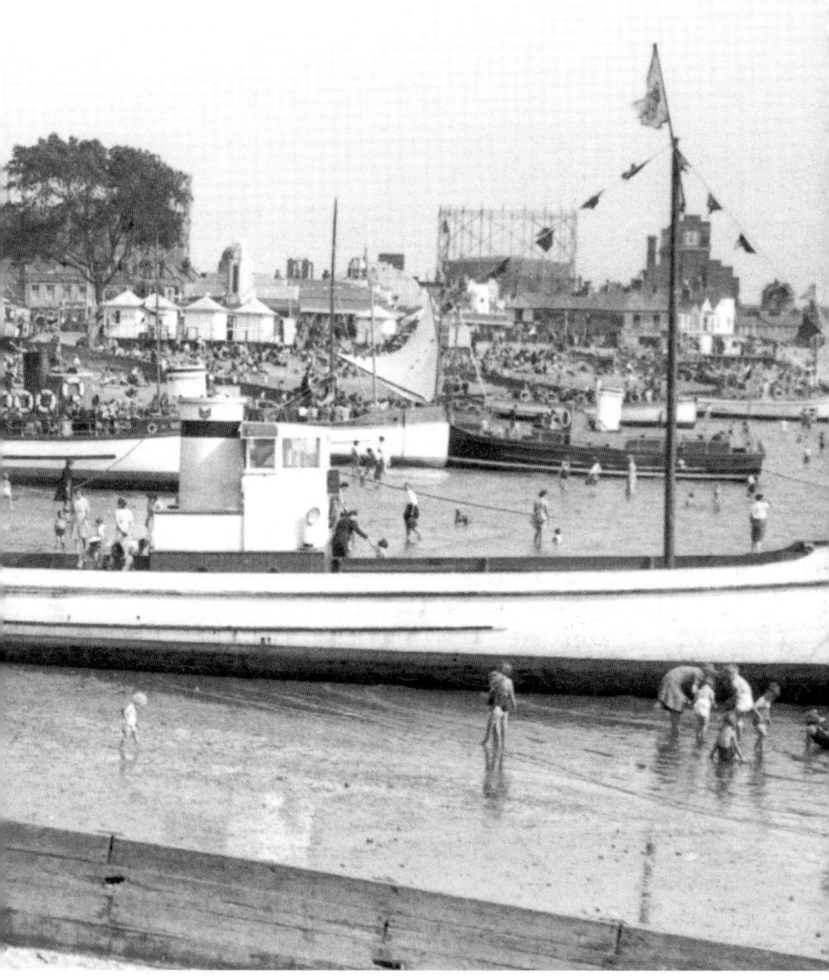

The lake is part of the moat surrounding the timber-framed manor house, once the home of the de Southchurch family. The central hall is open to the roof beams. A Tudor extension was added to the west of the building in 1560. Here we have an excellent view of part of the moat around the brick and wooden-framed manor house. At this time the building was still used as a public library. An imposing chimney rises above the left-hand wing of the building, whilst a smaller one can be seen to the right.

SOUTHEND

SOUTHCHURCH HALL, THE LAKE   c1950 / S155026

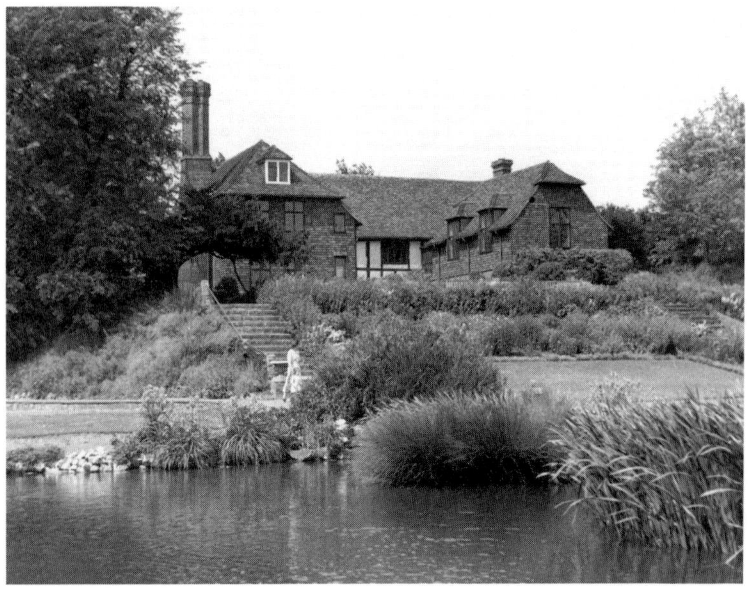

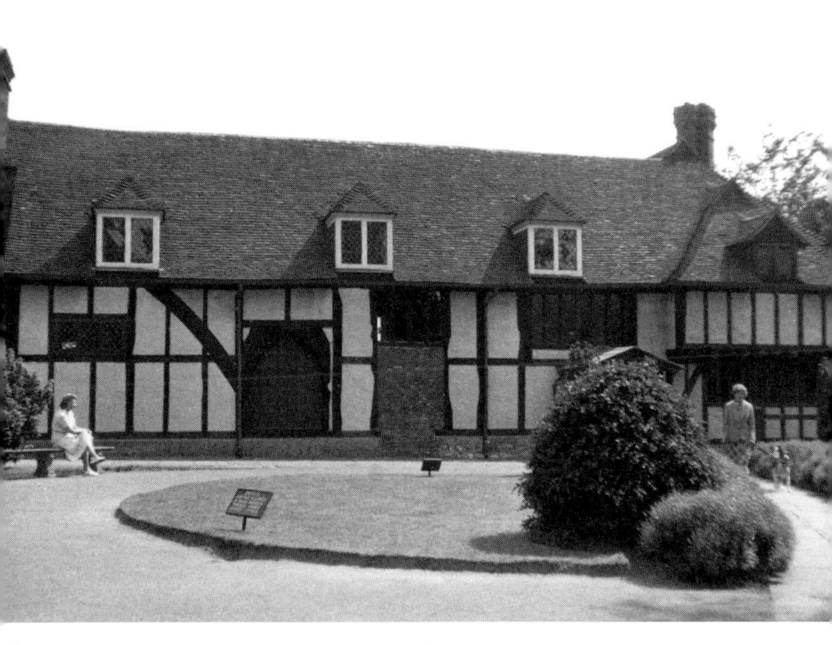

The well-known local Dowsett family gave this beautiful moated manor house to the town. It was restored in 1930 and opened as a library in 1931. The building dates from the late 13th to early 14th centuries and was opened as a museum in 1974.

SOUTHEND

SOUTHCHURCH HALL, THE LIBRARY   c1950 / S155028

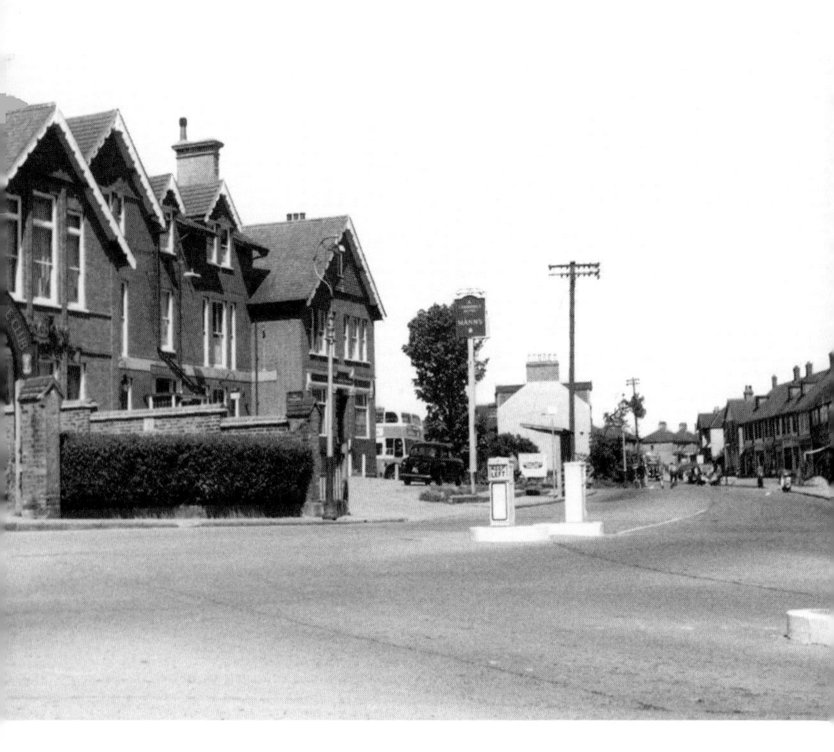

This wide junction seems to be ready for busier times to come. In the foreground stands the arch of the Conservative Club, with the solid brick-built Cambridge Hotel next door. The honey-pot style telegraph poles carry lines to the surrounding buildings.

SHOEBURYNESS

NESS ROAD   C1955 / S275022

SHOEBURYNESS

THE PROMENADE   c1955 / S275016

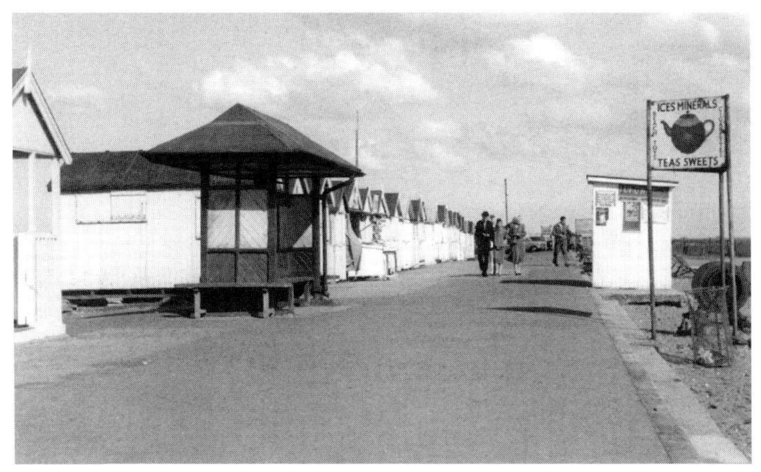

This imposing brick gateway, surmounted by a clock tower, was built 1860-62. A soldier stands to the right of the gate. The post box and telephone box must have been well used by residents at the camp. The Shoeburyness School of Gunnery was founded in the middle years of the 19th century.

SHOEBURYNESS
THE GARRISON CLOCK TOWER   C1955 / S275006

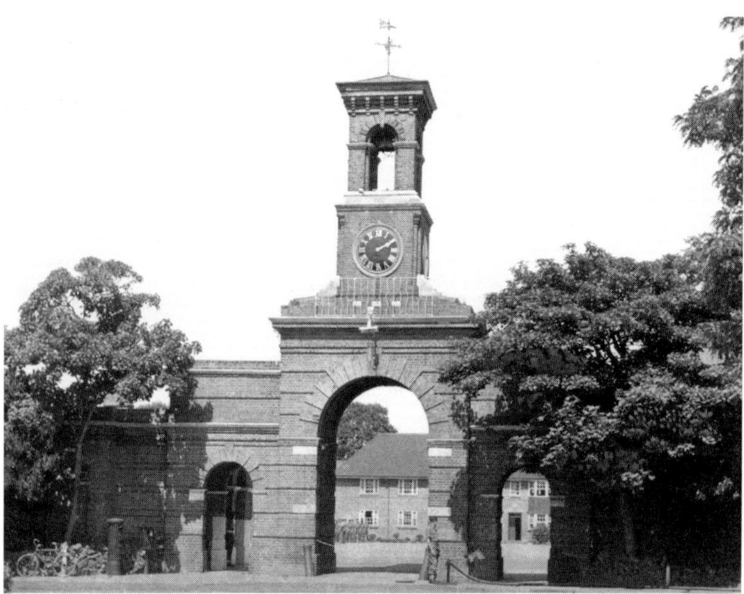

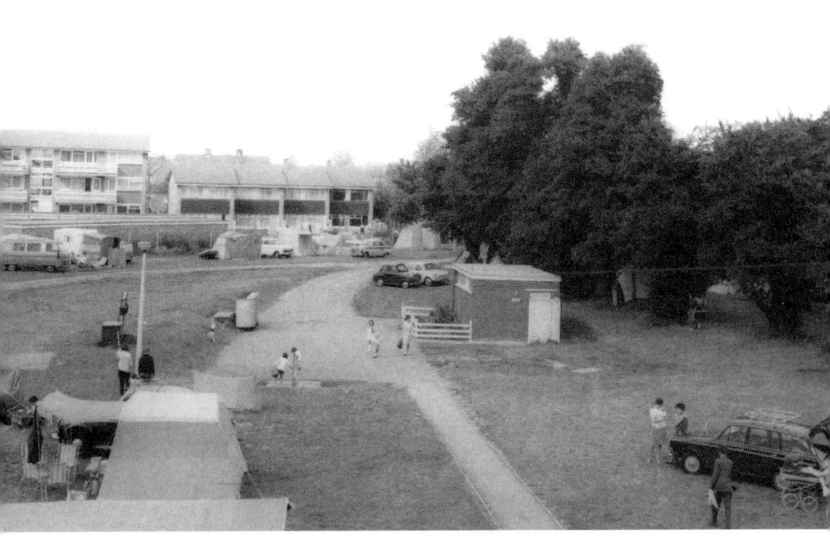

Camping was a popular, cheap way of spending a family holiday by the sea. The tent in the foreground has a large awning, a useful way of extending the living area. This site is close to a sand and shingle beach. Roof racks were frequently used to carry extra camping equipment.

SHOEBURYNESS

EAST BEACH TENT SITE   c1960 / S275095

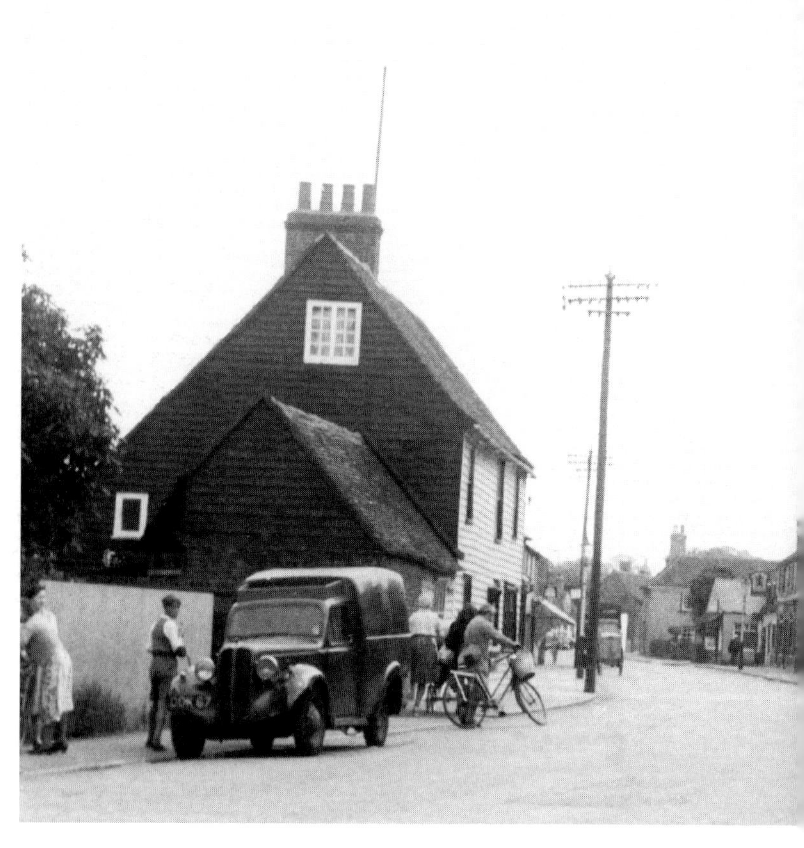

GREAT WAKERING

HIGH STREET C1950 / G100002

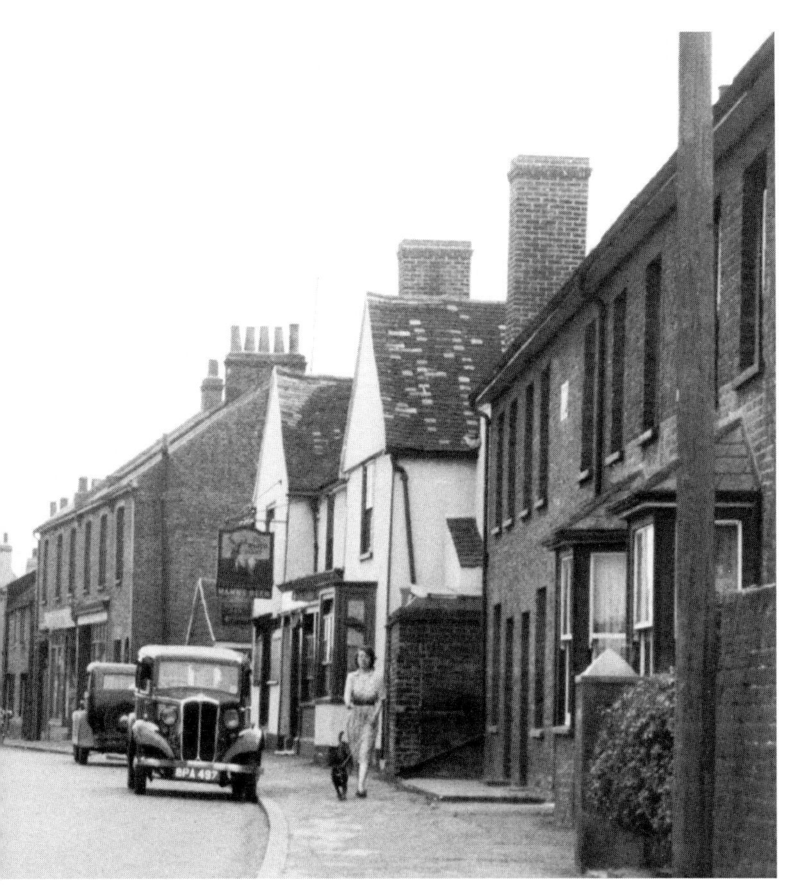

Wakering is noted for its low rainfall. In this picture we have a wide road and little traffic. On the left-hand side typical Essex weatherboard cottages survive, with the front door leading directly on to the street. The Lion and The White Hart public houses can be seen in close proximity on the right-hand side of the road, the latter, with its tiled roof, advertising Manns Beer.

Paglesham is a village of two parts, Church End and East End. In this picture the East End Post Office can be seen on the right, the one building in the row not faced with weatherboard. The small store facing the photographer also housed the Coastguard Reporting Officer. Both these buildings would have been of vital importance to the village at a time when many inhabitants had no personal transport. The buildings are still to be found close to The Plough and Sail public house, although no longer used for commercial purposes.

PAGLESHAM
THE STORES   c1955 / P143002

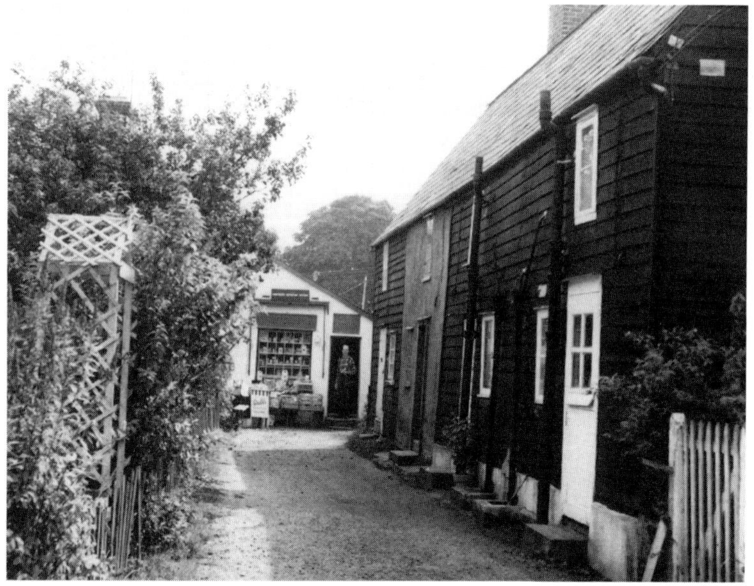

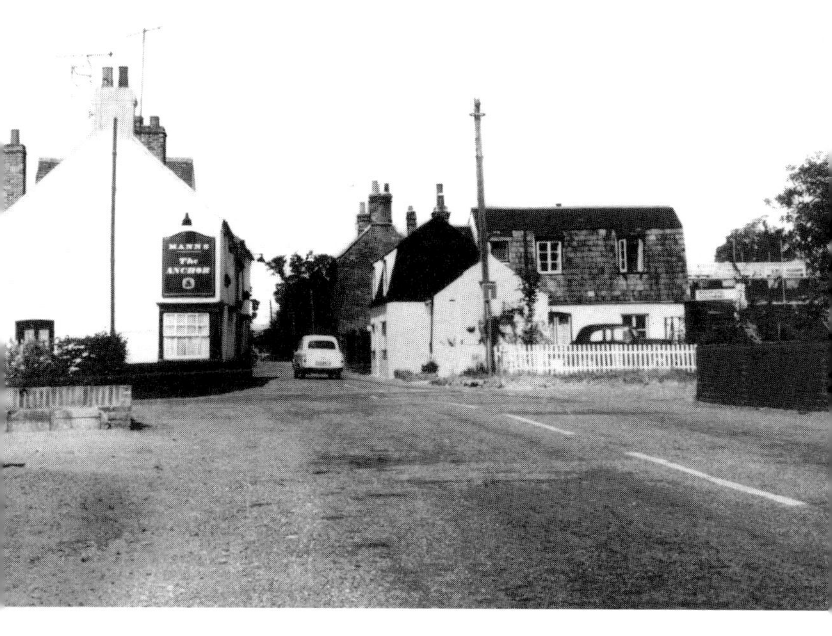

There is a timeless quality about this scene and little has changed over the years, apart from the type of car in use. The Anchor stands on the corner, proudly displaying its allegiance to Manns Beers. White's Lemonade is advertised outside the shop.

CANEWDON

HIGH STREET   C1955 / C236002

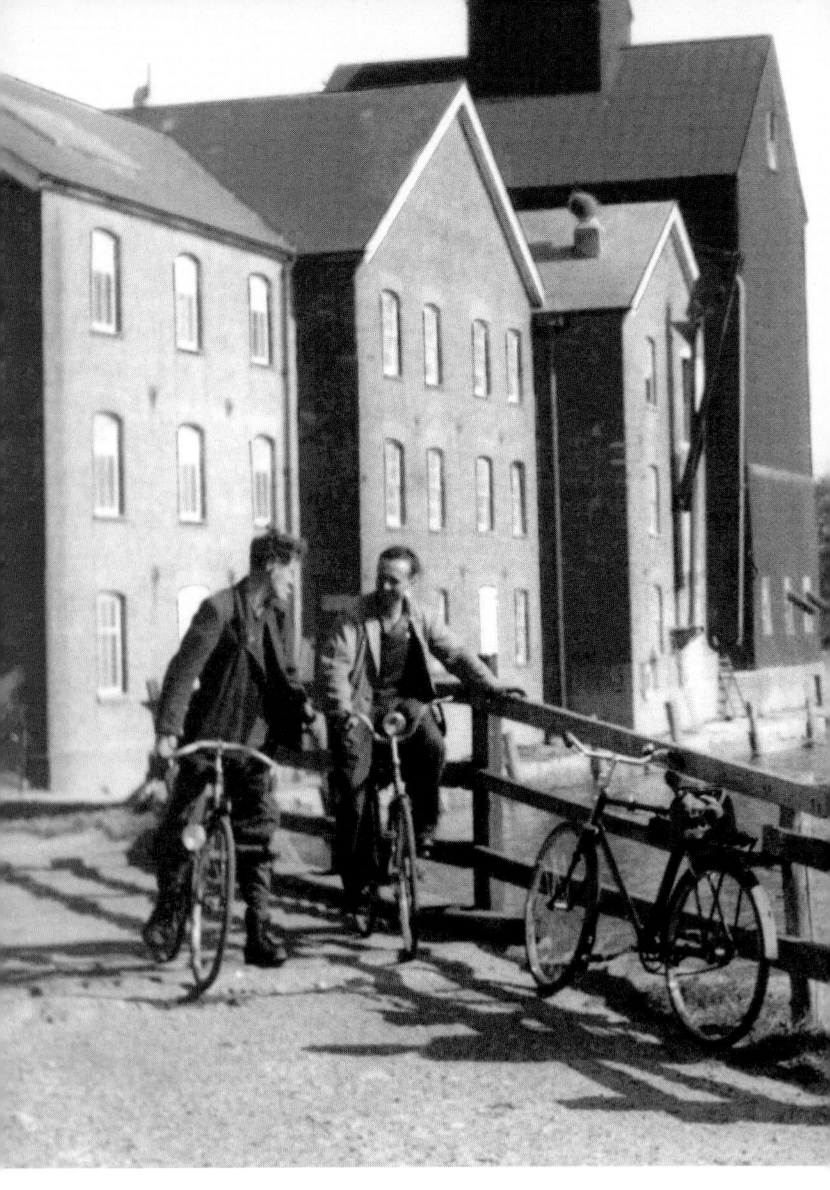

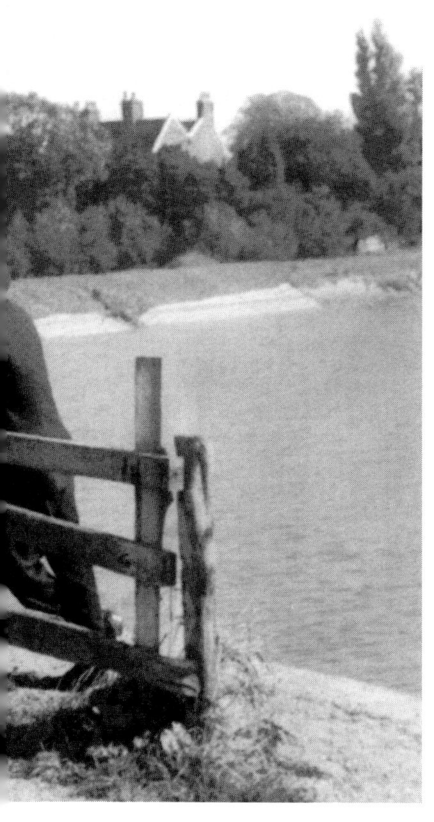

The bicycle was still a very important mode of transport when this photograph was taken. The brick-built buildings look as if they will last for another century at least. However, the huge Allied Flour Mill now stands on the site and very little of this scene remains.

ROCHFORD

STAMBRIDGE MILL

C1955 / R226011

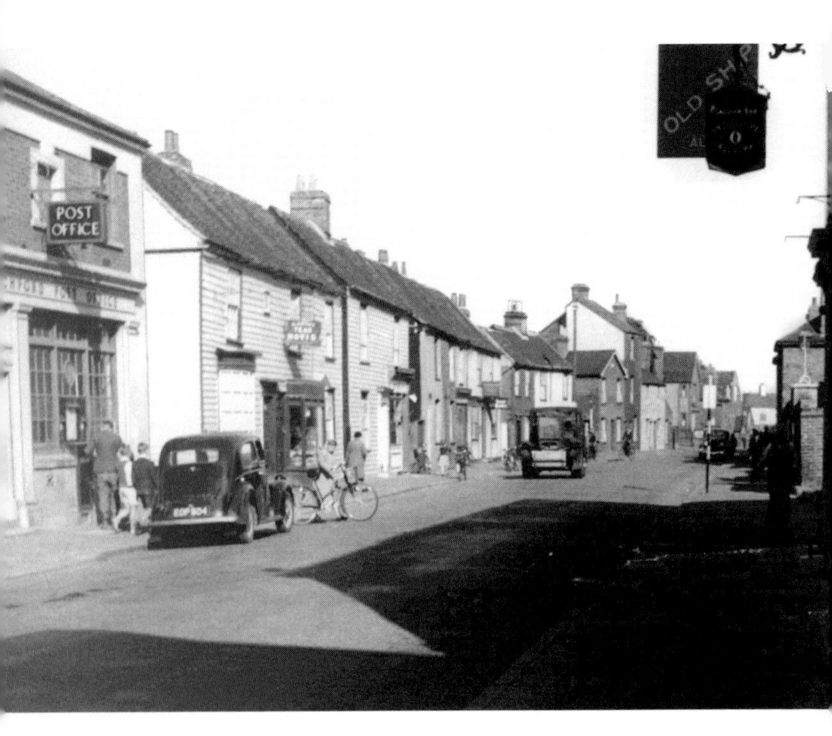

Here are more Essex weatherboard cottages with tiled roofs. Notice the sign for Teas and Hovis bread over one small shop. The reassuringly solid-looking Post Office is brick built and faces the Old Ship Inn. Straight-backed cars, complete with running boards, can be seen.

ROCHFORD

NORTH STREET   C1955 / R226003

ROCHFORD

MARKET SQUARE   C1955 / R226015

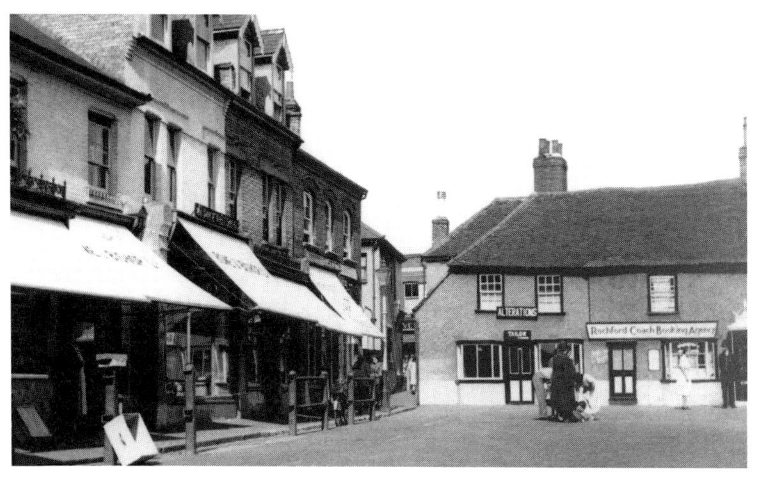

ROCHFORD

MARKET PLACE   C1965 / R226039

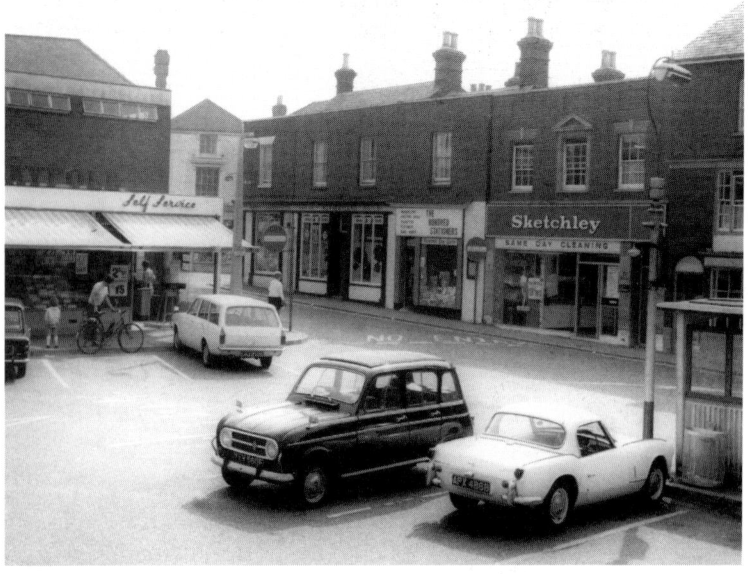

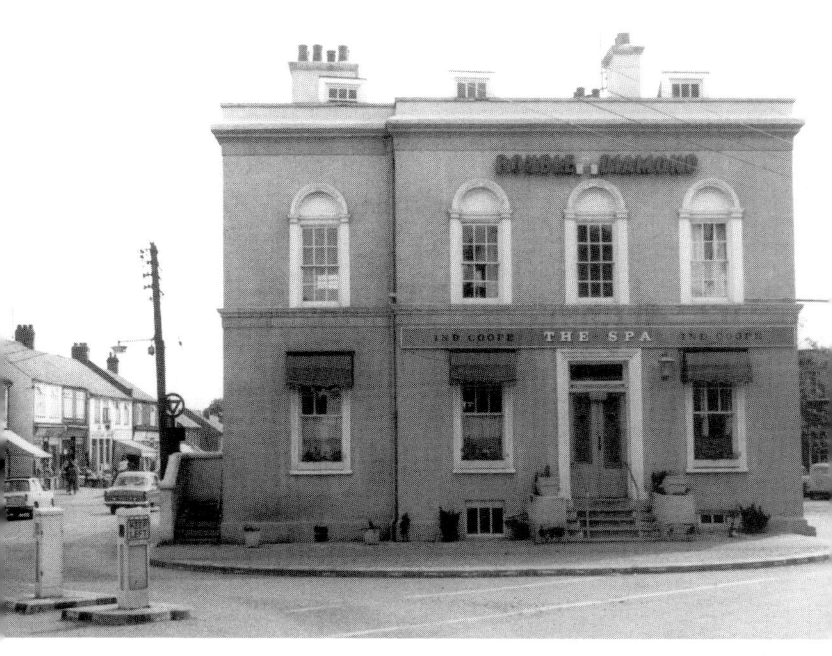

A spa was opened in Hockley in the early years of the 19th century and for some years was very successful, with many visitors coming to take the health-giving waters. This imposing Ind Coope hotel was built close by. The original spa building still exists in the road to the left of the picture.

HOCKLEY

THE SPA HOTEL   c1960 / H176035

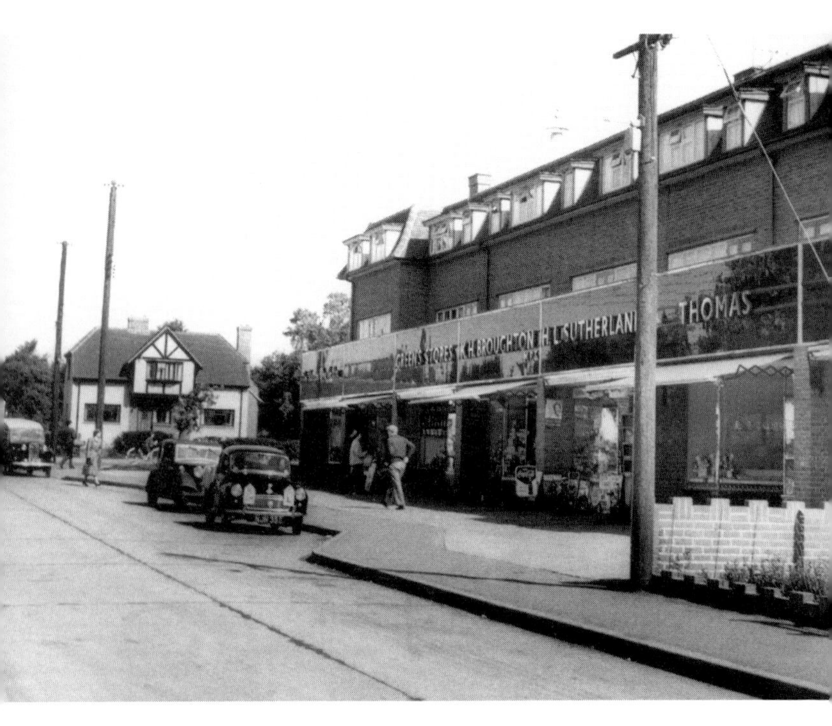

Continuing along the road containing the spa building, this parade of shops is to be found on the right-hand side. Hockley was a growing town by this time and a parade like this, typical of development in the 1950s, would have been well used. Shop names can be clearly seen on their shiny facia boards.

HOCKLEY

BROAD PARADE   c1955 / H176020

The village street shown in this picture is now a busy part of the town. The two cars, a motor cycle and one bicycle reflect a slower pace of life. The bank, with its solid door, is half hidden by a large tree. In the next building the International Store can be seen. This was a flourishing grocery chain at the time. The Crown Hotel proudly proclaims the sale of Manns Beer.

RAYLEIGH

THE VILLAGE   1951 / R224018

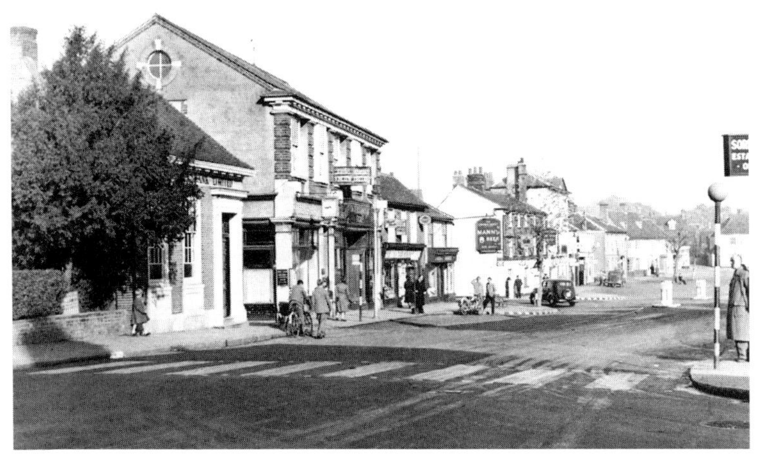

The Post Office building is solidly built of brick. Further along, on the left of the picture, the Salvation Army Chapel may be seen, with the car close by. The Co-operative Society advertisement proudly boasts that it has more than one thousand service points in London and Southend. The Southend Co-operative was founded in 1890 and later merged with the Stratford Co-operative Society.

RAYLEIGH

HIGH STREET   C1955 / R224009

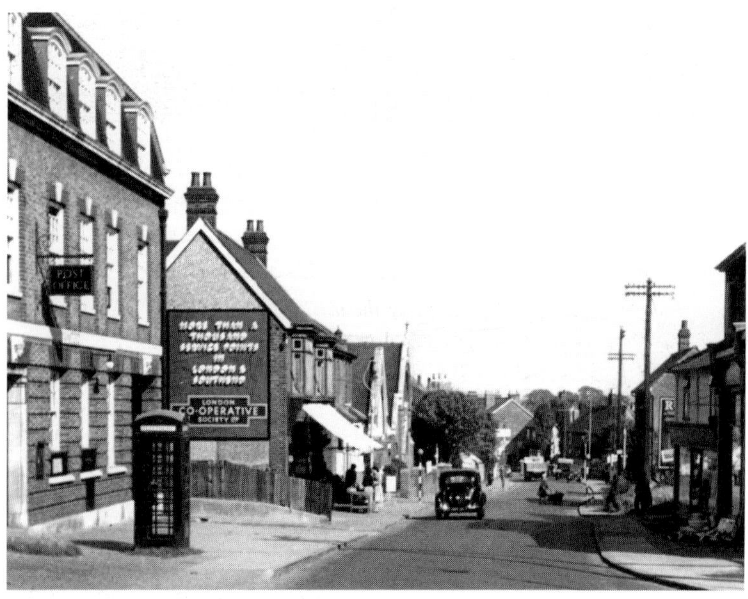

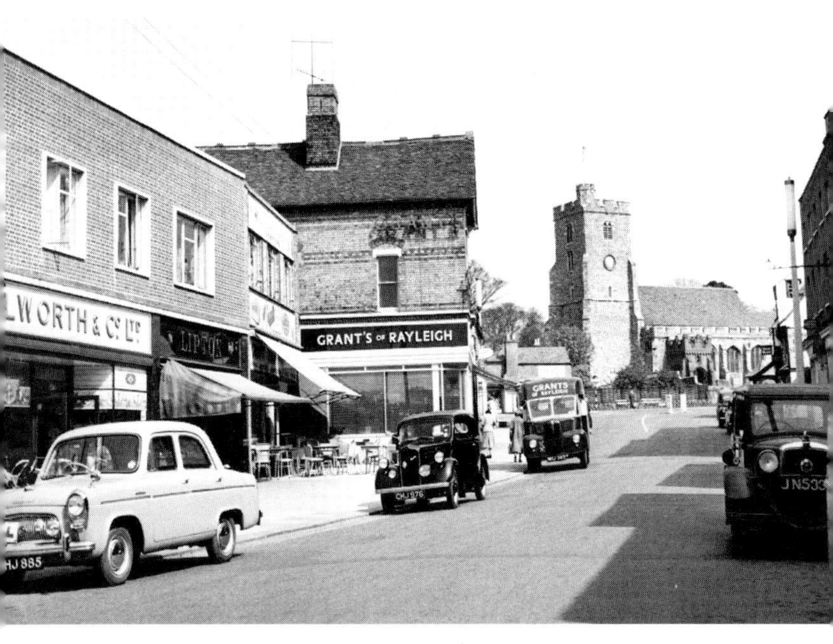

The imposing church of Holy Trinity dominates this scene. There are some Norman traces to be found in the chancel, although much of the building dates from the 15th century. The large porch is of brick. Only the mound of the town's once important castle remains. The road is wide with unrestricted parking. Woolworth's stands beside Lipton's, another well-known grocery chain. The A127 lies to the south of the town.

RAYLEIGH

TOWN CENTRE   1957 / R224027

INDEX

PLEASE HELP US BRING FRITH'S PHOTOGRAPHS TO LIFE

Our authors do their best to recount the history of the places they write about. They give insights into how particular towns and villages developed, they describe the architecture of streets and buildings, and they discuss the lives of famous people who lived there. But however knowledgeable our authors are, the story they tell is necessarily incomplete.

Frith's photographs are so much more than plain historical documents. They are living proofs of the flow of human life down the generations. They show real people at real moments in history; and each of those people is the son or daughter of someone, the brother or sister, aunt or uncle, grandfather or grandmother of someone else. All of them lived, worked and played in the streets depicted in Frith's photographs.

We would be grateful if you would tell us about the many places shown in our photographs—the streets with their buildings, shops, businesses and industries. Describe your own memories of life in those streets: what it was like growing up there, who ran the local shop and what shopping was like years ago; if your workplace is shown tell us about your working day and what the building is used for now. With your help more and more Frith photographs can be brought to life, and vital memories preserved for posterity.

We will gradually add your comments and stories to the archive for the benefit of historians of the future. Wherever possible, we will try to include some of your comments in future editions of our books. Moreover, if you spot errors in dates, titles or other facts, please let us know, because our archive records are not always completely accurate—they rely on 150 years of human endeavour and hand-compiled records.

So please write, fax or email us with your stories and memories. Thank you!

CHOOSE ANY PHOTOGRAPH FROM THIS BOOK

for your FREE Mounted Print. Order further prints at half price

Fill in and cut out the voucher on the next page and return it with your remittance for £2.50 for postage, packing and handling to UK addresses (US $5.00 for USA and Canada). For all other overseas addresses include £5.00 post and handling.
Choose any photograph included in this book. Make sure you quote its unique reference number eg. 42365 (it is mentioned after the photograph date. 1890 / 42365). Your SEPIA print will be approx 12" x 8" and mounted in a cream mount with a burgundy rule line (overall size 14" x 11").

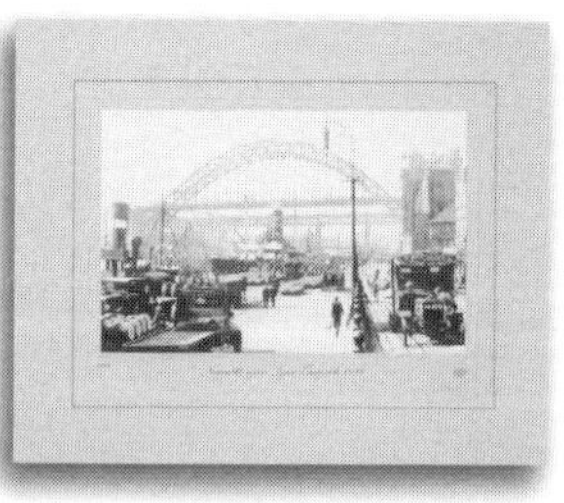

Mounted Print
Overall size 14 x 11 inches

Order additional Mounted Prints at HALF PRICE - If you would like to order more Frith prints from this book, possibly as gifts for friends and family, you can buy them at half price (with no extra postage and handling costs) - only £7.49 each (UK orders), US $14.99 each (USA and Canada).

> *** IMPORTANT!**
>
> These special prices are only available if you order at the same time as you order your free mounted print. You must use the ORIGINAL VOUCHER on the facing page (no copies permitted). We can only despatch to one address.

Have your Mounted Prints framed (UK orders only) - For an extra £14.95 per print you can have your mounted print(s) framed in an elegant polished wood and gilt moulding, overall size 16" x 13" (no additional postage).

FRITH PRODUCTS AND SERVICES

All Frith photographs are available for you to buy as framed or mounted prints. From time to time, other illustrated items such as Address Books, Calendars, Table Mats are also available. Already, almost 50,000 Frith archive photographs can be viewed and purchased on the internet through the Frith website.

For more detailed information on Frith companies and products, visit

www.francisfrith.co.uk

For further information, trade, or author enquiries, contact:

The Francis Frith Collection, Frith's Barn, Teffont, Salisbury SP3 5QP
Tel: +44 (0) 1722 716 376 Fax: +44 (0) 1722 716 881 Email: sales@francisfrith.co.uk

Voucher for FREE and Reduced Price Frith Prints

Do not photocopy this voucher. Only the original is valid, so please fill it in, cut it out and return it to us with your order.

Picture ref no	Page number	Qty	Mounted @ £7.49 UK @$14.99 US	Framed + £14.95 (UK only)	US orders Total $	UK orders Total £
1		1	**Free of charge***	£	$	£
2			£7.49 ($14.99)	£	$	£
3			£7.49 ($14.99)	£	$	£
4			£7.49 ($14.99)	£	$	£
5			£7.49 ($14.99)	£	$	£
6			£7.49 ($14.99)	£	$	£

Please allow 28 days for delivery

	US $	UK £
* Post & handling	$5.00	£2.50
Total Order Cost	US $	£

Title of this book . . . .

I enclose a cheque / postal order (UK) for £ . . . . $ . . . .
payable to 'Francis Frith Collection' (USA orders 'Frith USA Inc')

OR debit my Mastercard / Visa / Switch (UK) / Amex card / Discover (USA)
(credit cards only on non UK and US orders), card details below

Card Number

Issue No (Switch only)   Valid from (Amex/Switch)

Expires   Signature

Name Mr/Mrs/Ms . . . .

Address . . . .

. . . .

. . . .

Postcode/Zip. . . . . Country . . . .

Daytime Tel No . . . .   Valid to 31/12/06

PAYMENT CURRENCY: We only accept payment in £ Sterling or US $. If you are ordering **from any other country, please pay by credit card**, and you will be charged in one of these currencies.